US DESTROYERS
VS
GERMAN U-BOATS

The Atlantic 1941–45

MARK LARDAS

OSPREY PUBLISHING
Bloomsbury Publishing Plc
Kemp House, Chawley Park, Cumnor Hill, Oxford OX2 9PH, UK
29 Earlsfort Terrace, Dublin 2, Ireland
1385 Broadway, 5th Floor, New York, NY 10018, USA
E-mail: info@ospreypublishing.com
www.ospreypublishing.com

OSPREY is a trademark of Osprey Publishing Ltd

First published in Great Britain in 2023

© Osprey Publishing Ltd, 2023

All rights reserved. No part of this publication may be reproduced or
transmitted in any form or by any means, electronic or mechanical, including
photocopying, recording, or any information storage or retrieval system,
without prior permission in writing from the publishers.

A catalogue record for this book is available from the British Library.

ISBN: PB 9781472854100; eBook 9781472854124; ePDF 9781472854094;
XML 9781472854117

23 24 25 26 27   10 9 8 7 6 5 4 3 2 1

Maps by Bounford
Index by Angela Hall
Typeset by PDQ Digital Media Solutions, Bungay, UK
Printed and bound in India by Replika Press Private Ltd.

Osprey Publishing supports the Woodland Trust, the UK's leading woodland
conservation charity.

To find out more about our authors and books visit
www.ospreypublishing.com. Here you will find extracts, author interviews,
details of forthcoming events and the option to sign up for our newsletter.

Author's note
The following abbreviations indicate the sources of the illustrations used in
this volume:

AC – Author's Collection
NARA – National Archives and Records Administration
NOAA – National Oceanic and Atmospheric Administration
USNHHC – United States Naval History and Heritage Command

Other sources are listed in full.

Author's dedication
I would like to dedicate this book to my second and newest granddaughter,
Paula Grace, who arrived December 21, 2021.

Editor's note
In most cases imperial measurements, including nautical miles (NM), knots
(kn) and long tons, have been used in this book. For ease of comparison,
please refer to the following conversion table:

1 NM = 1.85km
1yd = 0.9m
1ft = 0.3m
1in = 2.54cm/25.4mm
1kn = 1.85km/h
1 long ton = 1.02 metric tonnes
1lb = 0.45kg

Front cover, above: Torpedoing of USS *Kearny*, October 1941. The
Norwegian tanker *Barfonn* is ablaze in the background. (Ian Palmer)
Front cover, below: Depth-charged U-boat in the Battle of the Atlantic. Note
that a Type VII U-boat was more likely to face this kind of attack at night.
(Ian Palmer)
Title page photograph: The Edsall-class destroyer escort USS *Martin H. Ray*
(DE-338) showing its HF/DF antenna. (USNHHC)

CONTENTS

INTRODUCTION

Between September 1941 and May 1945, United States Navy destroyers fought German Kriegsmarine ("War Navy") *Unterseeboote* – the U-boats. The battle opened on September 4, 1941, when USS *Greer* (DD-145), a Wickes-class flush-deck destroyer converted to anti-submarine warfare (ASW) duty, exchanged fire with *U-652*, a Type VIIC U-boat. The encounter took place in the western approaches to Iceland and was initiated when an RAF Coastal Command Lockheed Hudson maritime patrol bomber dropped depth charges on *U-652*. The U-boat's skipper, Oberleutnant zur See Georg-Werner Fraatz, unable to detect the Hudson, assumed *Greer* had been the attacker; *Greer* had in fact been tracking *U-652* on its sonar. In retaliation, *U-652* fired a torpedo at *Greer*, which then depth-charged the U-boat.

The final encounter occurred on May 6, 1945, the day after Germany surrendered. *U-881*, a Type IXC/40 U-boat, was attempting to line up a shot at the Casablanca-class escort carrier USS *Mission Bay* (CVE-59) when it was detected by USS *Farquhar* (DE-139), an Edsall-class destroyer escort screening *Mission Bay*. *Farquhar* attacked at 04:41:00, sinking *U-881*.

In between, there were thousands of encounters between US Navy destroyers and German U-boats, and between destroyer escorts and U-boats when the former began to operate in the Atlantic in April 1943. For ASW, destroyers and destroyer escorts can be considered interchangeable. Most encounters, like the combat between *Greer* and *U-652*, ended harmlessly, with neither side suffering damage. Others, like *U-881*'s encounter with *Farquhar*, had fatal consequences.

The U-boat was not inevitably the loser, however. The last US Navy warship sunk in the Battle of the Atlantic was USS *Frederick C. Davis* (DE-136), an Edsall-class destroyer escort that had survived three years of war, including a stint off the invasion beaches at Anzio on the western coast of Italy where it acted as a decoy for radio-controlled glide bombs. On April 24, 1945 *Frederick C. Davis* was tracking a U-boat contact, *U-546*, a Schnorchel-equipped Type IXC/40, which turned the tables on the destroyer escort, hitting it with a single acoustic torpedo. Hit at 08:40:00, *Frederick C. Davis* sank 15 minutes later. It was soon joined by *U-546*, attacked by the remaining eight destroyers in the hunter-killer group that *Frederick C. Davis* had been operating with.

Once or twice, an encounter proved fatal to both combatants. The Clemson-class flush-deck destroyer USS *Borie* (DD-215) served in the Neutrality Patrol in 1941. In 1943, along with several other sister ships converted for ASW duty, *Borie* was part of the destroyer screen for the Bogue-class escort carrier USS *Card* (CVE-11) hunting U-boats in the mid-Atlantic. On November 1, 1943, having detected the submerged *U-405*, *Borie* launched a depth-charge attack that forced the U-boat to the surface.

U-405, a Type VIIC U-boat, surfaced so close to *Borie* that the old four-piper could not depress its four 4in and one 3in guns sufficiently to engage the U-boat.

Kriegsmarine *U-bootsmänner* sweating out a depth-charge attack. The U-boat had to remain silent to evade detection and destruction; so did the crew. These men survived. Most depth-charge attacks were unsuccessful, but a U-boat only had to be unlucky once. (AC)

U-405 opened up on *Borie* with its deck guns. *Borie* responded with what it could – small-arms fire. Finally *Borie* rammed *U-405*, which sent the U-boat to the bottom. *Borie* damaged its bow when it rammed, however, and the battle was fought in a storm. Too badly damaged to tow to port, *Borie* was scuttled the next day.

These were typical of the encounters that occurred during the 45 months US Navy destroyers and destroyer escorts battled U-boats in the North Atlantic and surrounding waters. These battles, however, tended not to fit the common stereotype of battles fought between Allied destroyers and German U-boats. Novels like Nicholas Monsarrat's *The Cruel Sea* (1951), C.S. Forester's *The Good Shepherd* (1955), and Lothar-Günther Buchheim's *Das Boot* (1973) describe the battles fought on the North Atlantic's northern convoy routes. These involved convoys traveling between North America and Britain, or more rarely, between Britain and Gibraltar.

The battles fought on the routes taken by the British-bound SC and HX or the America-bound ON and ONS convoys were among the biggest and most important fought during the Battle of the Atlantic, but they were not typical of the battles in which the US Navy participated. This was not absolute: on October 31, 1941 the Clemson-class destroyer USS *Reuben James* (DD-245) was torpedoed and sunk by the

A crewman from the Clemson-class destroyer USS *Borie* (DD-215) is hoisted aboard the Bogue-class escort carrier USS *Card* (CVE-11) via a breeches buoy on November 3, 1943. *Borie* sank in a storm due to damage incurred ramming and sinking *U-405*. (AC)

Type VIIC U-boat *U-552* while escorting HX 156 from Newfoundland to Iceland. However, this was during the period of the Neutrality Patrol.

After the United States entered World War II in December 1941, the battlefield changed. The Battle of the Atlantic was no longer confined to the eastern North Atlantic, but instead included the western Atlantic Ocean, the North American seaboard, the Gulf of Mexico and Caribbean Sea, and the waters off South America. Moreover, the US Navy suddenly had massive naval commitments in the Pacific Ocean, against Japan.

US Navy destroyers were largely withdrawn from the northern convoy routes. Eventually, the US presence in these convoys was limited to the US Coast Guard, often manning vessels equivalent to destroyers, including destroyer escorts lent to the US Coast Guard. The Royal Canadian Navy assumed responsibility for convoys on the western half of those routes while Britain's Royal Navy took charge of the eastern half. US warships tended to operate under the command of British or Canadian leaders. *The Good Shepherd*'s Commander Ernest Krause was a rare (and fictional) exception.

Instead, the US Navy initially patrolled the waters along the North American coast, the Caribbean, and the Gulf of Mexico. After November 1942 they took responsibility for the convoys taking the central North Atlantic routes, between Norfolk, Virginia and Gibraltar, and on into the Mediterranean. The US Navy was fighting a different type of war against U-boats than that being fought by the Royal Navy or Royal Canadian Navy – geography dictated it.

The US Navy rarely fought "wolf packs," which could only be engaged in areas relatively close to French and Norwegian U-boat bases and in areas with large convoys, namely the northern convoy routes. Wolf packs could have been deployed against US–Gibraltar convoys in the approaches to Gibraltar, but these were heavily patrolled by Allied maritime patrol aircraft and therefore best avoided by U-boats. That meant most US destroyer and destroyer-escort encounters with U-boats were typically with individual U-boats.

Another difference was US destroyers and destroyer escorts were more frequently used offensively against U-boats than defensively protecting convoys. Although 1942 destroyer sweeps hunting U-boats were helter-skelter, by 1943 destroyers and destroyer escorts were used in hunter-killer groups centered around escort carriers. The escort carriers' aircraft would hunt out U-boats, with the destroyers sent to sink the U-boats that submerged before aircraft could sink them.

This book presents those battles, and highlights what made them unique. While in 1942 it appeared the U-boats were invincible, by 1944 they were on the run.

CHRONOLOGY

1935

June 18 Anglo-German Naval Agreement signed, permitting Germany to build U-boats.

June 29 Kriegsmarine commissions Type IIA SM *U-1*, its first U-boat.

1941

September 4 *Greer* Incident. *Greer* and *U-652* exchange fire.

October 17 *Kearny* torpedoed by *U-568*.

October 31 *Reuben James* sunk by *U-552*.

Two *U-bootsmänner* in the control room of a U-boat. They are operating the depth controls that determined the depth at which the U-boat should be. (AC)

December 7 United States attacked by Japan at Pearl Harbor and other locations in the Pacific.

December 11 Germany declares war on United States.

1942

January 12 Operation *Paukenschlag*, the first attack by U-boats on the American coast, begins when Type IXB *U-123* sinks the unescorted British cargo steamship *Cyclops*.

February 28 *Jacob Jones* sunk off the Delaware Capes by Type VIIC *U-578*.

February German U-boats begin using the four-rotor Enigma cipher machine. The Allies can no longer read U-boat radio traffic.

April 14 *U-85* sunk by *Roper*, the first U-boat sunk by US Navy destroyers.

May 28 *U-568* sunk off Torbruk by Royal Navy warships.

August US Navy depth charges modified to allow 600ft depth settings.

November 16 Gleaves-class destroyers USS *Woolsey* (DD-437), USS *Swanson* (DD-443), and USS *Quick* (DD-490) sink *U-173* as it attempts attacking Operation *Torch* shipping.

1943

March 5 A hunter-killer group, with the escort carrier *Bogue* and five flush-deck destroyers, departs Norfolk, becoming the first US Navy task group to hunt U-boats.

March 13 Type VIIC *U-575* becomes the first U-boat to be sunk by US Navy destroyers in the Mediterranean.

April	First destroyer escort enters service in the Battle of the Atlantic.
August 1	*Zaunkönig* (Wren) acoustic homing torpedo enters service. It is called GNAT (German Naval Acoustic Torpedo) by the Allies.
November 1	*U-405* rammed and sunk by *Borie*. The destroyer is scuttled the next day.
December 24	Wickes-class destroyer USS *Leary* (DD-158), hit by a *Zaunkönig* torpedo fired by Type VIIC *U-275*, becomes the last US Navy destroyer sunk by U-boats.

1944

February 16	Destroyer escorts accompany an escort carrier hunter-killer task force for the first time.
March 17	Gleaves-class destroyer USS *Corry* (DD-463) and Cannon-class destroyer escort USS *Bronstein* (DE-109) sink Type IXC/40 *U-801*, the first time a destroyer escort participates in sinking a U-boat.
May 5	Buckley-class destroyer escort USS *Fechteler* (DE-157), torpedoed and sunk by Type VIIC/41 *U-967* while escorting a convoy in the Mediterranean, becomes the first US Navy destroyer escort sunk by U-boats.
May 6	In a wild battle involving a boarding action by German *U-bootsmänner*, *Buckley* rams and sinks Type IXC *U-66*.
May 19	Gleaves-class destroyers USS *Niblack* (DD-424) and USS *Ludlow* (DD-438) sink Type VIIC *U-960*, the last U-boat sunk by US Navy destroyers in World War II.
May 29	*U-549* sinks *Block Island*, and is subsequently sunk by *Eugene E. Elmore*.
June 4	Four destroyer escorts from TG 22.3 force *U-505* to the surface and capture it.

July 5	Type XB *U-233* is forced to the surface by Cannon-class destroyer escorts USS *Baker* (DE-190) and USS *Thomas* (DE-102) and sunk by gunfire, becoming the only Type XB U-boat sunk by US Navy escort warships.

1945

April 24	*Frederick C. Davis* sunk by *U-546*, which is subsequently sunk by six destroyer escorts.
April 30	Karl Dönitz succeeds Adolf Hitler as head of the Third Reich.
May 4	Dönitz orders the Kriegsmarine to cease all offensive action.
May 5	Dönitz orders the Kriegsmarine to cease all hostilities.
May 6	*Farquhar* sinks *U-881* – the last U-boat sunk by the US Navy.
May 8	Germany surrenders. War in Europe (and Battle of the Atlantic) ends.
May 23	Third Reich dissolved by the Allies. Dönitz is arrested.
May 29	Blackout in Atlantic Ocean ends. Ship navigation lights again used.
August 17	Type VIIC *U-997*, the last U-boat still at sea, arrives in Argentina and surrenders.

Although torpedoes were rarely used by destroyers and destroyer escorts against U-boats, they were fired on occasion against surfaced U-boats. No U-boat was sunk by torpedoes fired by a US Navy surface warship, although one, *U-537*, was torpedoed and sunk by the Gato-class submarine USS *Flounder* (SS-251) on November 10, 1944 in the South China Sea. This is a torpedoman aboard a destroyer escort. (AC)

DESIGN AND DEVELOPMENT

THE DESTROYER AND THE DESTROYER ESCORT

The destroyer emerged between 1892 and 1894 to counter the threat torpedo boats presented to large warships. This torpedo-boat destroyer was built to drive off torpedo boats. An oceangoing warship, it could keep up with the battle fleet and was fast enough to engage and sink torpedo boats before they endangered the battle line. The torpedo-boat destroyer, large enough to carry torpedoes and a better sea boat than the smaller torpedo boat, soon replaced the latter type. The name "torpedo-boat destroyer" was shortened to "TBD" or simply "destroyer."

The first generation of destroyers had coal-fired, reciprocating steam engines. Their maximum speeds ranged from 25 to 31kn; they displaced between 350 and 600 tons, and they carried two torpedo tubes, one or two guns between 65mm and 88mm in caliber, and two to four light guns between 20mm and 50mm.

Second-generation destroyers arrived between 1904 and 1912, incorporating steam turbines and oil fuel. Turbine engines provided greater power per unit weight than the triple-expansion

A U-boat plows through open water in the North Sea. This view is from the bridge, looking forward. (AC)

reciprocating steam engines and the oil fuel had higher specific energy than coal, which eliminated the need for stokers to fuel the boiler. Additionally, burning oil created no ash to remove from the firebox.

The third generation of destroyers emerged between 1913 and 1916, adding geared propulsion. Turbine efficiency increases with greater turbine speed, while a propeller is most efficient at a relatively slow speed. At high shaft speeds, marine propellers force dissolved air in water out of solution. Gas bubbles form and collapse, creating turbulence. The propeller pushed against air, not water.

Destroyer size and speed increased with each generation. The first generation barely made 24kn. Slow second-generation destroyers could make 28kn, with faster classes reaching 36kn. The size of second-generation destroyers increased to 500–750 tons. Torpedo batteries had four to eight torpedo tubes, and the ships carried up to four main guns, of up to four inches in bore.

The third generation was larger still: 750–1,100 tons. They were as fast as the smaller ships, better sea boats, and carried more torpedo tubes. The final class of US "1000-tonner" destroyers, the Sampson class of 1915, carried 12 21in torpedo tubes in triple mountings, and could reach 29.5kn.

In 1915, the United States wanted a super-destroyer, superior to those of other nations, with high speed, excellent seakeeping, and good range. The super-destroyer was to fill the scout cruiser role when necessary. Range was critical because the US Navy operated their destroyers in oceans. The rest of the world's navies intended their destroyers to operate in seas.

The result was a flush-decked, four-smokestack (pipe) design displacing 1,125 tons, 310ft long on the waterline, with a 30kn top speed. It could travel 2,500nm at 20kn. As designed, it carried 12 21in torpedo tubes in four broadside mounts and a quadruple 4in/50-gun main battery. It could accompany the battle line across half an ocean, scout out the enemy, and then fight. A total of 273 were built between 1917 and 1922.

Submarine and aircraft emerged as threats during World War I. Submarines, especially German U-boats, were an ever-present and deadly peril. Fleet actions, by contrast, were relatively rare. Something had to deal with U-boats. Due to their speed and agility – and their relative disposability, compared to battleships or cruisers – that task fell to destroyers.

The Caldwell, Wickes, and Clemson classes of flush-deck destroyers were the first mass-produced destroyers built for the US Navy. They served into World War II, becoming early-war leaders in the fight against the U-boats. (USNHHC)

The Farragut-class destroyer was the first new US Navy destroyer design in over a dozen years. It introduced the 5in/38 dual-purpose gun, which formed the main battery of US Navy destroyers through the Korean War. This is USS *Aylwin* (DD-355). (AC)

US destroyers that served in World War I, including the flush-deck classes, were hastily retrofitted with anti-submarine weapons. The most common was the depth-charge rack permitting depth charges to be rolled off the stern of a destroyer. Some destroyers were also fitted with Y-guns, Y-shaped depth-charge launchers, which projected depth charges off either side of the destroyer.

ASW became a permanent part of the destroyer mission. For flush-deckers, still primarily intended to accompany the battle line, this form of warfare was improvised. They lacked space for more than a pair of depth-charge racks mounted on the stern or stowage for adequate quantities of depth charges.

The sheer number of flush-deckers froze US destroyer development for a decade. The next generation of US destroyers finally appeared in the mid-1930s, their design constrained by the terms of the London Naval Treaty of 1930, a naval limitations agreement between Britain, France, Italy, Japan, and the United States limiting the number and size of destroyers allowed navies. Both submarines and aircraft had grown in capability since World War I. New destroyer designs factored that in. Yet in 1931, when design work on the next generation of US destroyers began, the destroyer's main role was as an auxiliary to the battle line. Anti-aircraft and anti-submarine capabilities were secondary.

The first destroyer class built after the flush-deckers were the Farraguts. Although equipped with sonar, as built they lacked depth-charge racks or throwers. They had two quadruple centerline 21in torpedo tubes and a main battery of four 5in/38 dual-purpose guns. The guns were a concession to the aircraft threat, but they were also capable against surface ships. Top speed of the Farragut-class destroyers was 36kn, but due to naval treaty limitations they displaced only 1,500 tons.

Although they were 20 percent larger than the flush-deckers, the Farraguts were also 20 percent smaller than desired by the Navy Board. They became the template for 1,500-ton and 1,650-ton pre-war destroyer designs. Along with the flush-deckers, these destroyers fought the Battle of the Atlantic. Larger and more capable wartime-construction destroyers, designed and built after naval treaty limitations expired, went overwhelmingly to the Pacific.

As the 1930s drew to a close, the US Navy became more focused on the threats posed by both aircraft and submarines. The limited number of battleships and cruisers operated by enemy nations' fleets put an emphasis on reducing the numbers of these ships through submarine ambush or aerial attack by torpedo bombers. Aircraft capability was increasing at rates that had to be frightening to naval officers. The US Navy began emphasizing the ASW and anti-aircraft roles destroyers would play, realizing the opportunities for surface torpedo attacks would be scarce.

USS *EUGENE E. ELMORE* (DE-686)

A Rudderow-class destroyer escort, *Eugene E. Elmore* was one of 447 destroyer escorts commissioned in the United States Navy. These vessels were designed for the Royal Navy specifically to fight U-boats. They were magnificent at that job, but not much else. In the Atlantic they were in their element. The Rudderow class differed from the earlier Buckley class (and other earlier destroyer-escort classes) mainly in armament. They carried two 5in/38 guns instead of the three 3in/50 guns of the earlier ships. As with earlier classes their engines ran generators to power the electric motors which drove the vessels. *Eugene E. Elmore* had a short career. Commissioned in December 1943, it escorted convoys in the Atlantic until November 1944. Thereafter it served in the Pacific until November 1945. It was decommissioned in May 1946, remaining in reserve until broken up in 1969.

USS *Eugene E. Elmore*

Displacement	1,450 tons
Dimensions	Length 306ft (overall); beam 36ft 10in; draft 9ft 8in
Machinery	General Electric steam turbo-electric drive engine developing 50,000shp
Speed	24kn
Range	5,500nm at 15kn
Fuel	Oil
Crew	15 officers, 168 enlisted
Armament	Three 21in torpedo tubes (1×3) and three 21in torpedoes; two 5in/38 guns (2x1); four 40mm Bofors guns (2x2); ten 20mm/70 AA guns (10x1); one Hedgehog projector; eight K-gun depth-charge throwers; two depth-charge racks

Destroyer anti-aircraft capabilities were good. New-construction main batteries for all destroyers after 1936 were 5in/38 dual-purpose guns, perhaps the finest heavy anti-aircraft gun of World War II; but it was also a highly effective weapon against surface vessels, including submarines. Light and medium batteries were wanting, however, especially on older construction.

ASW capability was more problematic. Some destroyers lacked even depth-charge racks. Depth charges likely to sink a submarine required destroyers to drop a larger pattern, which included launching them sideways by projectors, such as the Y-gun used in World War I. Y-guns could not be placed on new-construction destroyers, however, so the US Navy created the K-gun, which fired depth charges in one direction. With a smaller footprint, K-guns could be mounted along the sides of the destroyer.

Although both light anti-aircraft guns and ASW weapons could be added, part or all of the torpedo battery or even a main gun turret had to be removed to provide space and weight for new weapons; this was viewed as acceptable. Starting in 1939 the US Navy began modifying older destroyers and altering new construction to improve destroyers' anti-aircraft and ASW capabilities. The additional light and medium anti-aircraft guns also improved destroyers' ASW effectiveness, especially against surfaced U-boats.

Surviving flush-deck destroyers went through the most extensive conversions, with 27 converted to ASW destroyers. Two sets of torpedo tubes and all 4in guns were removed, replaced with six 3in/50 dual-purpose guns and six K-guns. The addition of six 20mm single guns further improved anti-aircraft protection.

Similar, if less extreme, conversions were made on newer pre-war destroyers. Depth-charge racks were added to destroyers lacking them. Often one or two sets of torpedo tubes were landed, replaced with K-guns and 20mm and 40mm anti-aircraft guns. This conversion process accelerated after the US entered World War II.

Radar, shipboard High-Frequency Direction Finding (HF/DF or "Huff-Duff"), and combat-information centers (CICs) were introduced during World War II. These all had to be retrofitted into pre-war construction, during the war. Also added to some destroyers was the Hedgehog projector. Developed during the war, it fired 24 contact-fused anti-submarine projectiles ahead of the firing vessel.

During the war, the US Navy developed a specialized anti-submarine destroyer, the destroyer escort. An austere destroyer, it was 290–306ft long (depending on class), 1,360 or 1,730 tons displacement, and had a top speed of either 21 or 24kn. Half were diesel-powered, as steam turbines were in short supply. Most used electric motors to drive the propellers, thus eliminating the need for gearing.

The Gleaves class was the last generation of destroyers designed before the expiration of naval limitations treaties. Many served in the Atlantic, fighting U-boats, including USS *Niblack* (DD-424), shown here during acceptance trials. (USNHHC)

Destroyer escorts were built with one center-mount triple torpedo tube, but this was often removed to increase the number of anti-aircraft guns. Their main battery was either two 5in/38 guns in turrets or three 3in/50 open-mount guns. In addition to depth-charge racks, they had eight depth-charge projectors, and a Hedgehog projector. They were also equipped with two to six 40mm and six to 12 20mm anti-aircraft guns. Construction started on the first destroyer escort in September 1941 and they began arriving for US Navy service in February 1943. They were deadly against Type VII or Type IX U-boats, but were too slow to be effective against Type XXI U-boats.

In 1941–42, most of the destroyers assigned to the Atlantic were the old flush-deckers or the then-new Benson-class and Gleaves-class destroyers. As the war went on, these remained in service in the Atlantic, joined by the first of the destroyer escorts in 1943. By the start of 1945 most flush-deck destroyers had been withdrawn from ASW duty, replaced by destroyer escorts or Benson- and Gleaves-class destroyers freed from duty in the Pacific by the arrival of later, larger wartime-construction destroyers. Although a few of the war-construction Fletcher- and Allen B. Sumner-class destroyers ended up in the Atlantic, these vessels had little contact with U-boats.

USS *Kearny*	
Displacement	1,630 tons
Dimensions	Length 348ft 3in (waterline); beam 36ft 1in; draft 11ft 10in
Machinery	Four Babcock & Wilcox boilers; two Westinghouse geared steam turbines on two shafts developing 50,000shp
Speed	37.4kn
Range	6,500nm at 12kn
Fuel	Oil
Crew	16 officers, 260 enlisted
Armament	Ten 21in torpedo tubes (2×5) and ten 21in torpedoes; five 5in/38 guns (5x1); six .50in machine guns (6x1); two depth-charge racks

USS *KEARNY* (DD-432)

USS *Kearny* was a Gleaves-class destroyer (also called the Benson-Livermore class). Launched March 9, 1940 and commissioned September 13, 1940, it became part of the Neutrality Patrol almost immediately after completing its shakedown cruise. *Kearny* was typical of Atlantic destroyers during World War II. Initially assigned because they were the newest destroyers available, they remained in the Atlantic to allow more-capable new construction to go to the Pacific. This plate depicts *Kearny* as it appeared in October 1941, when it was part of the Neutrality Patrol. At the time it lacked the 20mm guns or the radar and HF/DF gear it acquired later in the war. There were wide variations in Gleaves-class anti-aircraft and ASW armament due to wartime modification.

THE GERMAN U-BOAT

The modern submarine – powered by an internal combustion engine while surfaced and an electric motor while submerged – emerged during the last decades of the nineteenth century. John P. Holland, an Irish immigrant to the United States, built his first submarine in 1878 and continued developing his designs over the next two decades. In 1900 the US Navy purchased Holland's most advanced design, *Holland IV*, becoming the first navy in the world to commission a submarine.

A 54ft-long, football-shaped spheroid with a 10ft diameter, *Holland IV* displaced 74 tons submerged and 64 tons on the surface and had a maximum diving depth of 75ft. It could travel at 6kn on the surface and only slightly slower (5.5kn) submerged. The crew worked and lived in its cylindrical pressure hull, which had external ballast tanks attached that could be filled with water to submerge or emptied (using compressed air) to surface.

Surfaced, *Holland IV* used a 45hp gasoline motor that powered batteries. These ran a 75hp electric motor, propelling the submarine when submerged. It had a single 18in torpedo tube and carried three torpedoes. While primitive, *Holland IV* was the ancestor for all future submarines for the next 50 years. All incorporated the basic features of *Holland IV*.

Britain, France, Russia, Japan – and Germany – soon acquired submersible warships. Krupp in Germany built its first U-boat in 1903, but the private venture failed to attract the interest of the Kaiserliche Marine (Imperial Navy) and it was sold to Russia. The Kaiserliche Marine purchased its first U-boat, SM *U-1*, in 1906. It was powered by a two-stroke kerosene (or paraffin) engine, had a top speed of 10.8kn, and a range of 1,500nm, but it still had only one torpedo tube and three torpedoes.

Just four years later, *U-19* entered service with the Kaiserliche Marine. It displaced 640 tons surfaced and 824 tons submerged. Measuring 210.5ft long, with a 20ft beam and a 24ft height, it had a test depth of 50m (164ft) and a 9,700nm surfaced range, and could reach 15.4kn surfaced and 9.5kn submerged. It had four 50cm (19.7in) torpedo tubes (two forward and two aft) and carried six torpedoes, and had three deck guns: one 88mm, one 105mm gun, and one 37mm. Instead of engines fed by volatile gasoline or kerosene, it had two MAN eight-cylinder diesel engines producing 1,700hp. The two engines powered two AEG electric motors generating 1,184shp.

SM *U-1* (shown) was the first submarine purchased by the Kaiserliche Marine. Although it had paraffin-fueled engines instead of diesels, it was the model for all subsequent German U-boats. (USNHHC)

U-19 was the template for all subsequent U-boats designed and built through 1943. By the end of World War I, Imperial Germany had two U-boat types, the UB-III class and the U-93 class, that were analogous to the later Type VII and Type IX U-boats, which formed the backbone of the Kriegsmarine's World War II U-boat forces.

The UB-III U-boats were considered coastal boats, yet were two-thirds' scale analogs to the Kriegsmarine Type VII U-boats. With an overall length of 55.3m (181ft 5in) and a maximum breadth of 5.8m (19ft, the pressure hull was 40.1m [131ft 6in] long and 3.9m [12ft 9in] in diameter), the UB-IIIs displaced 516 tons surfaced and 651 tons submerged. They had a crew of 35 men and carried five torpedo tubes (four forward, one aft), ten torpedoes, and an 88mm deck gun with 160 rounds for it. They could reach a maximum speed of 13.6kn surfaced and 8kn submerged, had a range of 9,040nm surfaced at 6kn, and a test depth of 75m (246ft). These were very capable U-boats, 88 of which were built during World War I.

The U-93-class U-boat design could have served as a downscaled Kriegsmarine Type IX U-boat. Oceangoing submarines intended for Atlantic patrols, they displaced 838 tons surfaced and 1,000 tons submerged, and were 71.55m (234ft 9in) long with a 6.3m (20ft 8in) beam. (The pressure hull was 56m [183ft 9in] with a 4.15m [13ft 8in] diameter.) They had a crew of 39, and carried six torpedo tubes (four bow, two stern), 16 torpedoes, and a 105mm deck gun with 140 rounds for it. With a maximum speed of 16.8kn surfaced and 8.6kn submerged, they had a range of 9,000nm at 8kn surfaced. Twenty-four U-93-class U-boats were commissioned in World War I.

Germany ended the war with the reputation of building the world's best submarines and operating them more effectively than any other nation. They were so good the Treaty of Versailles, which ended World War I, barred Germany from building, having, or operating U-boats.

In 1922 the Reichsmarine (Realm Navy, the Kaiserliche Marine's successor) evaded these limitations by establishing Ingenieurskantoor voor Scheepsbow (IvS) den Haag, a submarine design office, in the Netherlands, a country neutral during World War I. IvS, supposedly a commercial company, was funded by the Reichsmarine and soon designed and sold submarines for export. The company's first sales were to Turkey, of two submarines that were built in 1927 using the UB-III design as the basis.

IvS soon went beyond updating World War I designs. Between 1927 and 1933 the company created three submarine designs later used by Germany in World War II. The first was a boat built by Spain in 1929–30, *Submarino E-1*, which was sold to

IvS spent the inter-war years designing U-boats in the Netherlands for other European countries. The company's designs were later used by the Kriegsmarine. The *Vetehinen*, built for Finland, served as the prototype for the Type VII U-boat. (AC)

17

Turkey in 1935, where it served under the name *Gür* until 1947. It was an oceangoing vessel, intended for long-range independent patrols. The design re-emerged in Germany in 1936 as the Kriegsmarine's Type IA U-boat. Only two were built, *U-25* and *U-26*. An upgraded version became the Type IX U-boat.

The next two IvS designs were built by Finland, newly independent after World War I. One, commissioned in Finland as *Vesikko*, was the prototype for the Type II coastal U-boat. The other became the Finnish Vetehinen-class submarines, the prototype for the Kriegsmarine's Type VII U-boats. Therefore, when Germany discarded the Treaty of Versailles limitations in 1936, it already had the three basic U-boat designs it would use during World War II. The three designs would remain in production through 1944.

The Type II U-boats were the smallest of the three designs, displacing 254 tons surfaced and 303 tons submerged. By August 1939 they were being retired to training and played no part in the Battle of the Atlantic fought by the US Navy. The various Type VII and IX U-boats built were the main opponents US Navy destroyers and destroyer escorts fought. Over 690 Type VIIs and nearly 200 Type IXs were commissioned during World War II and were vastly superior to their World War I counterparts.

The Type VII and IX U-boats had test depths of 230m (750ft). They could reach speeds of 17–18kn on the surface, and 7.6kn submerged. Their diesel engines and electric motors were highly reliable. Both types carried 55.3cm (21in) torpedoes, with warheads three times the weight and four times the power of the 45.5cm (17.7in) torpedoes carried by World War I U-boats. The Type IX U-boats had phenomenal range – the Type IXD could almost circumnavigate the globe without refueling.

Both the Type VII and Type IX designs had limitations. They needed to remain surfaced at least eight hours a day to recharge the batteries that drove the electric motors used when submerged. They were designed to primarily operate surfaced, but Kriegsmarine doctrine called for nighttime attacks on Allied convoys while surfaced to enable U-boats to use their superior surface speed and avoid sonar detection. This worked well in the war's opening years, but by 1943 most Allied ASW vessels had radar.

Type VII and IX U-boats relied on silence to avoid detection, but by using active sonar or radar to detect enemy ships, Allied warships were able to detect and track U-boats. That limited U-boats to relying on visual observation over a 5–15-mile radius on the surface. This in turn forced U-boats to rely on constant radio communication to coordinate attacks on convoys. By mid-1943, however, many ASW warships had HF/DF equipment, allowing them to detect and locate broadcasting U-boats. Only after the Kurier burst-transmission system was installed on U-boats did that risk of detection diminish.

The Type IX U-boat was designed as a long-range cruising U-boat, intended to operate independently, rather than in wolf packs. Although the US Navy fought Type VII U-boats, its main quarry was the Type IX. (USNHHC)

Germany also produced a Type X minelaying U-boat and a Type XIV supply U-boat. Large by German standards – around 1,700 tons surfaced and up to 2,300 tons submerged – they were used for mid-ocean supply of Type VII and IX U-boats. The Type X had only two stern tubes for minelaying and defensive use. The Type XIV had no torpedo tubes. These vessels avoided surface warships, with which an encounter always ended badly. Of the eight Type X and ten Type XIV U-boats built, 13 were sunk by aircraft and three by destroyers or destroyer escorts.

Types VII and XI U-boats were modified and improved during the course of World War II, but their late 1920s–early 1930s design limited the scope of this work. The Kriegsmarine knew that it needed a new design to overcome the disadvantages created by the Allies' use of radar and ASW aircraft, but they did not start ordering replacements for these pre-war U-boats designs until 1943. These were the *Electroboot* – Type XXI and Type XXIII U-boats. They were designed to operate submerged, reaching speeds up to 17kn. They could recharge their batteries submerged, using a Schnorchel to provide air to their diesel engines. They arrived too late for service, however: of the 118 Type XXI and 61 Type XXIII U-boats commissioned by the Kriegsmarine, only eight conducted patrols before the war ended, all in 1945 and in sectors of Royal Navy responsibility.

THE "MILCH COWS"

U-boats, especially the Type VII, were designed to fight in the North Sea and Atlantic waters around Britain. The capture of French and Norwegian ports allowed them to operate in the mid-Atlantic, astride convoy routes connecting Britain to North America. However, they lacked the endurance to fight at the far side of the Atlantic or off South America. They could reach these battlefields, but remain only a few days before returning home.

The Kriegsmarine began stationing supply boats in the mid-Atlantic, to provide combat U-boats with fuel, food, and torpedoes. At first, captured foreign submarines were used. Prior to World War II, Germany started building four large Type XB minelaying U-boats. These 2,100-ton vessels were deployed as "Milch Cow" supply U-boats, starting in 1941. The scheme worked so well, four more Type XBs were built and ten Type XIV purpose-built supply U-boats were commissioned. They operated in the central Atlantic, far from land-based aircraft.

The Milch Cows became prime targets for US Navy hunter-killer groups, and they proved highly vulnerable to both the carrier aircraft and destroyers fielded by these groups. All but two were lost by the war's end, seven of which were sunk attempting to run the Bay of Biscay. US Navy hunter-killer groups bagged another eight Milch Cows, including three sunk by destroyers or destroyer escorts.

Type XB U-boat *U-233* as it is being attacked by the Cannon-class destroyer escorts USS *Baker* (DE-190) and USS *Thomas* (DE-102). (USNHHC)

OPPOSITE

Locations of key clashes between
U-boats and US destroyers,
1941–45

THE STRATEGIC SITUATION

The Avro Anson was RAF Coastal
Command's main ASW aircraft in
World War II's opening year. It
was, however, incapable of
sinking a U-boat, a failure that
allowed Germany to mount a
highly successful campaign
against merchant vessels with
U-boats. (AC)

There should never have been a Battle of the Atlantic in World War II. At most, it should have been a minor effort, ended before the United States entered the war, focused on hunting down Kriegsmarine warships and auxiliary cruisers. That it exploded into the Western Allies' biggest campaign of the early-war years was unexpected to both sides. The U-boat peril became the only issue that ever really frightened Winston Churchill during World War II.

The final year of World War I saw Imperial Germany's U-boat campaign against merchant shipping crushed under a combination of depth charges, convoys, and aircraft. By the 1930s, ASDIC (or sonar: sound navigation and ranging) had been added to the mix to allow underwater tracking of submarines. Sonar was common on destroyers and other anti-submarine warships by the time Germany invaded Poland in September 1939.

Convoys proved decisively effective in defeating individual U-boats. Simply forming convoys reduced the opportunities for a U-boat to find a target by 95–98 percent by concentrating shipping into a small patch of ocean. A lone U-boat could not use its deck guns against a convoy of armed merchantmen. It had to expend scarce torpedoes.

While aircraft had difficulty detecting submerged U-boats, they could cover vast ocean areas quickly,

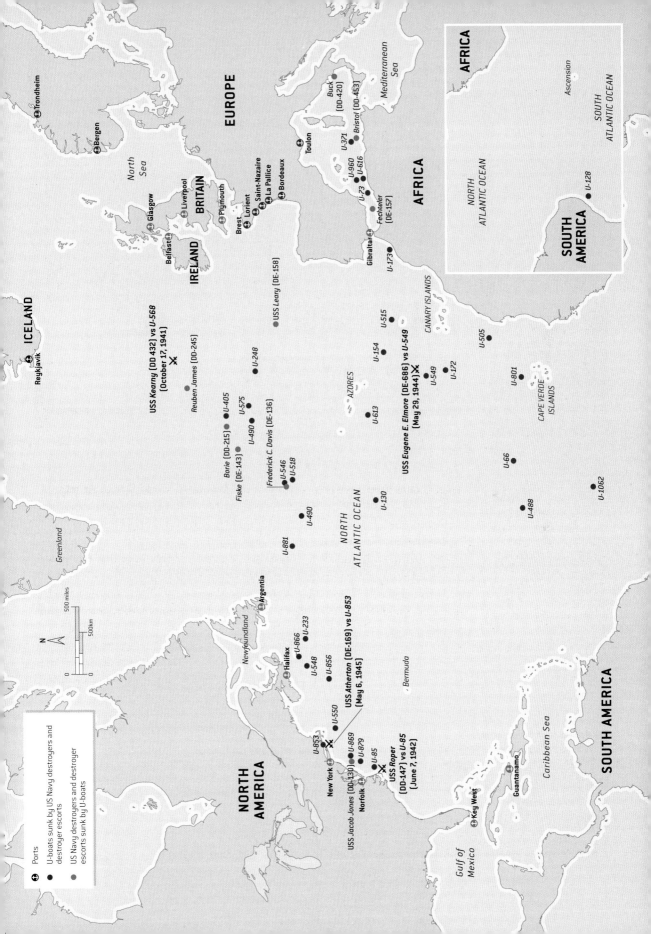

AFRICA

Ascension

SOUTH ATLANTIC OCEAN

NORTH ATLANTIC OCEAN

U-128

SOUTH AMERICA

EUROPE

Trondheim

Bergen

North Sea

Glasgow
Liverpool
Belfast
IRELAND
BRITAIN
Plymouth
Brest
Lorient
Saint-Nazaire
La Pallice
Bordeaux

Mediterranean Sea

Buck
(DD-420)
Bristol (DD-453)
Toulon
U-371
U-960
U-616
U-73
Fechteler
(DE-157)

AFRICA

Gibraltar
U-173

CANARY ISLANDS

U-515

USS Leary (DE-158)

U-154

USS Eugene E. Elmore (DE-686) vs U-549
(May 29, 1944)
U-549
U-172

U-505

U-613

AZORES

U-801

ICELAND

Reykjavik

USS Kearny (DD 432) vs U-568
(October 17, 1941)

Reuben James (DD-245)

U-248

U-405
U-575
U-490
Borie (DD-215)
Fiske (DE-143)
Frederick C. Davis (DE-136)
U-546
U-518

U-130

U-490

U-881

U-66

U-488

U-1062

CAPE VERDE ISLANDS

Greenland

500 miles
500km

N

0
0

NORTH ATLANTIC OCEAN

NORTH AMERICA

Newfoundland

Argentia

Halifax
U-866
U-233
U-548
U-856

USS Atherton (DE-169) vs U-853
(May 6, 1945)

Bermuda

U-550

U-853
U-869
U-879
U-85

USS Jacob Jones (DD-130)
New York
Norfolk

USS Roper
(DD-147) vs U-85
(June 7, 1942)

Gulf of Mexico

Key West

Guantanamo

Caribbean Sea

SOUTH AMERICA

Ports

U-boats sunk by US Navy destroyers and destroyer escorts

US Navy destroyers and destroyer escorts sunk by U-boats

A common sight during the years from 1930 through 1943 was shipwrecked mariners, forced into lifeboats and life rafts after their ships were sunk by U-boats. These three men are being rescued after spending 83 days on a life raft. (AC)

detecting and attacking surfaced U-boats. Even if aircraft attacks missed, they forced U-boats to submerge, drastically reducing their effectiveness. U-boats had to remain surfaced to recharge batteries – and for scouting. Armed aircraft made it impossibly difficult for U-boats to hunt out merchant convoys.

No navy, including Germany's Kriegsmarine, built submarines in the 1930s intending to use them as commerce raiders. Their mission was envisaged as being to accompany their navies' surface fleets. Acting as advance scouts, they were to ambush the enemy's line of battle to weaken it prior to fighting the decisive surface action expected by all navies. Two things changed this doctrine and the Battle of the Atlantic.

The first was that Britain's Royal Air Force (RAF), focused almost exclusively on strategic bombing, neglected to obtain aircraft or weapons capable of sinking U-boats. Their standard anti-submarine weapon when the war started, the 100lb anti-submarine bomb, was completely ineffective against U-boats. Yet it was the only weapon the Avro Anson, the RAF's main ASW aircraft, could carry. The RAF also lacked an air-droppable depth charge that could be carried by most of its ASW aircraft until May 1941.

The need for a strong, effective RAF Coastal Command should have been obvious. Britain depended on imports to feed its population and its industries. Without control of the Atlantic, Britain would starve. It almost had in World War I. Yet, two decades later, the RAF was unable to perform the critical ASW function. Instead, anti-submarine efforts fell entirely on the Royal Navy's overstretched ASW warships: destroyers, sloops, and corvettes.

The second factor was the commander of the Kriegsmarine's U-boats in 1939, Konteradmiral (Rear Admiral) Dönitz, who believed he could overcome the difficulties created by sonar and convoys. To defeat sonar he trained his U-boat crews to attack surfaced, at night. Surfaced U-boats were invisible to sonar, and at night a surfaced U-boat's silhouette was so small as to make it invisible – but surface ships were easily spotted from a U-boat's bridge.

To find convoys, Dönitz set up picket lines of U-boats to locate surface ships as they crossed the Atlantic. He also planned coordinated attacks by groups of U-boats on convoys, called *Rudeltaktik* ("pack tactics," an alternative name for the wolf pack), but did not implement the tactics until late 1941 because he had too few U-boats at his disposal.

It did not matter. The new tactics, combined with completely ineffectual Allied ASW aircraft, led to what U-boat captains called *Die Glückliche Zeit* ("the Happy Time") from July 1940 until April 1941. Bold U-boat commanders snuck into

U-BOAT ANTI-ESCORT TACTICS

When faced with a US Navy destroyer or destroyer escort, a U-boat could make one of three appropriate responses. It could dive to evade, fire a conventional electric or steam-powered torpedo, or (after August 1943) fire an acoustically guided *Zaunkönig* torpedo. Each course had advantages and disadvantages.

1. **Dive to Evade**: As soon as detection by a destroyer is discovered, dive the U-boat to the maximum depth possible, changing direction when diving. Through most of 1942 this was the safest course, unless the destroyer was too close for the U-boat to reach safety. US depth charges could not be set below 300ft, and a combat U-boat had a 230m (750ft) test depth, out of range even after 600ft settings were possible. Since the destroyer lost sonar contact as it attacked with depth charges, by changing direction the U-boat could avoid being under the depth charges. (This advantage was lost if attacked with contact-fused projectiles.)

2. **Fire a Conventional Torpedo:** Wait near the surface and fire one or more conventional torpedoes at the destroyer. Since they were small, elusive targets, this required a four-torpedo spread for best effect. This wasted torpedoes that could otherwise be used on merchantmen. If running from the attacker only one or two torpedoes could be fired from stern tubes. If the torpedo missed — highly likely with one torpedo — the destroyer would depth-charge the U-boat before it dived to 300ft.

3. **Fire a Homing Torpedo:** Keep a *Zaunkönig* in a stern tube. Fire it at the oncoming destroyer as you dive using a sound bearing when at 60m (200ft). Hope the *Zaunkönig* blows the stern off your pursuer. If it misses, there is time enough to reach 200m before the destroyer reaches the U-boat.

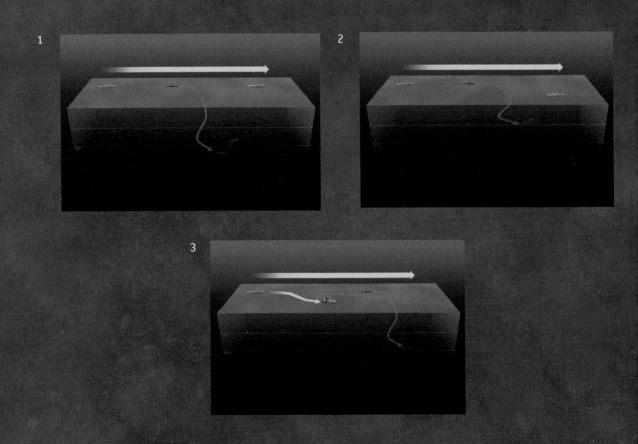

convoys at night. They fired all their torpedo tubes, then submerged, hiding from sonar with the wrecks of the ships they had hit and sunk in the attack. U-boats sank merchant ships in wholesale lots.

Reinforcing early-war success, Germany started building new U-boats in large numbers. It would take until 1942 before the new U-boats built as a result of this increased production entered combat, but the U-boats' 1939 and 1940 successes led Germany into a new commerce warfare campaign. This was Dönitz's "tonnage war," based on sinking ships of the merchant marine faster than they could be replaced.

The British finally began to bring the U-boats under control in April 1941. More destroyers and more effective attacks led to the destruction of three prominent U-boats that month. Better and more numerous ASW vessels, combined with effective RAF Coastal Command ASW aircraft and the arrival of air-droppable depth charges, were beginning to bring the U-boats to heel.

President Franklin D. Roosevelt believed if Britain were forced to surrender to Germany, the United States would become Germany's next target. Wishing to keep the war as far away from North America as possible, he began supporting Britain. In September 1940, he brokered a deal whereby the United States traded 50 flush-deck destroyers for US bases in British possessions in the Western Hemisphere.

Roosevelt next sponsored legislation allowing the United States' armed forces to "lend" fuel, supplies, and military equipment, including aircraft and ships, to Britain and other nations at war. The materiel was a free loan if it was returned at the war's end. Only materiel not returned was subject to payment. Known as the Lend-Lease Act, the legislation passed on March 11, 1941.

German gains in March and April 1941 led Roosevelt to further support Britain. The United States accepted an invitation from the Danish Government-in-Exile to serve as protector of Greenland, then a Danish colony. The US Navy then declared a

Eternal vigilance was required in the fight against U-boats. Here two men from a gun's crew stand watch, searching for U-boats while two others sleep by the gun so as to be ready at a moment's notice if they are required to man it. (AC)

belligerent exclusion zone, forbidding any belligerent power from approaching closer than 25 miles of Western Hemisphere land masses – unless they had colonies. This permitted Britain, France, Denmark, and the Netherlands unrestricted passage, while excluding German and Italian aircraft and naval vessels.

On May 27, Roosevelt declared an unlimited national emergency. The US military was "to repel any and all acts or threats of aggression directed toward any part of the Western Hemisphere." The United States military went on a war footing. The US Navy established the Neutrality Patrol to enforce the exclusion of German and Italian warplanes and warships from Roosevelt's declared neutrality zone. While the Neutrality Patrol included battleships and aircraft carriers, the backbone of the patrol was a collection of Benson- and Gleaves-class and flush-deck destroyers patrolling the sea lanes between Iceland and North America's Atlantic Seaboard for German U-boats.

This could have been interpreted as an act of war by Germany but Hitler, preoccupied by his upcoming invasion of the Soviet Union, chose to ignore the provocation. He also ignored the provocation when, in June–July 1941, the United States took over from Britain the responsibility of defending Iceland. Although the US was neutral, this act allowed Britain to use Iceland as an air and naval base, while barring the Germans, who had no desire to expand the Atlantic battlefield. Dönitz could put no more than 50 U-boats at sea on any given day through the middle of September 1941, and they were fully occupied on operations in the North Atlantic between Iceland and Britain.

This armed neutrality brought U-boats and US Navy destroyers into frequent contact. Tensions escalated in the fall, following three incidents. On September 4, *Greer* exchanged fire with *U-652*. No hits were scored by either side but, as a result of this incident, US Navy ships began escorting Atlantic convoys from the Eastern Seaboard to the Mid-Ocean Meeting Point south of Iceland, with inevitable consequences.

On October 17 the Gleaves-class destroyer USS *Kearny* (DD-432), escorting the eastbound convoy SC-48, was torpedoed by *U-568*. Damaged, the destroyer limped safely to Iceland. Two week later, on October 31, *Reuben James*, escorting HX-156, was torpedoed and sunk by *U-552*.

The United States and Germany spent the next 40 days diplomatically glowering at the other. Each side hoped and feared the other would declare war on them. Even *Reuben James*'s sinking did not sufficiently sway public opinion in the United States to lead to a declaration of war on Germany. Hitler wanted his U-boats in the Mediterranean and Norwegian seas, not the western Atlantic, because the latter was the extreme operational limit of the Type VII and the early Type IX U-boats.

Then, on December 7, 1941, the stalemate was broken. The Empire of Japan attacked British, Dutch, Commonwealth, and US holdings in the Pacific and Far East. This included an attack on the US naval base at Pearl Harbor, Hawaii Territory. The following day, the United States declared war on Japan. Three days later, on December 11, Germany and Italy declared war on the United States. The Battle of the Atlantic was entering a new and different phase, but one thing had not changed – the Allies had to win the battle or else lose the war.

US NAVY ANTI-SUBMARINE TACTICS

A destroyer had two basic means of attacking a submerged U-boat: dropping depth charges on it, or dropping anti-submarine projectiles if it had a Hedgehog or Mousetrap projector installed. Regardless of the method used, an attack followed the same basic pattern shown below:

1. A destroyer makes sound contact with a U-boat. It comes to battle stations.

2. The destroyer closes on the U-boat, maintaining sound contact until it can attack.

3. If the destroyer opts for a depth-charge attack, it steams over the U-boat's presumed location (presumed because as it passes over, it loses sonar contact) and drops a pattern of depth charges, guessing at the U-boat's depth. If it misses, it cannot attack again until the noise disturbance of the depth charges dies away several minutes later.

4. If the destroyer opts for a Hedgehog attack, it fires a ring of projectiles at the U-boat, firing ahead of the destroyer, maintaining sonar contact while attacking. No depth setting is needed and the projectiles only explode on contact. If the first attack misses, the destroyer can make a new attack almost immediately.

Despite the drawback of depth charges, captains were more familiar with them and initially used them in preference to projectiles. If nothing else, they sounded impressive. Captains started using projectiles after being ordered to report why they were not using them, and continued using them after discovering they were five times more likely to sink a U-boat.

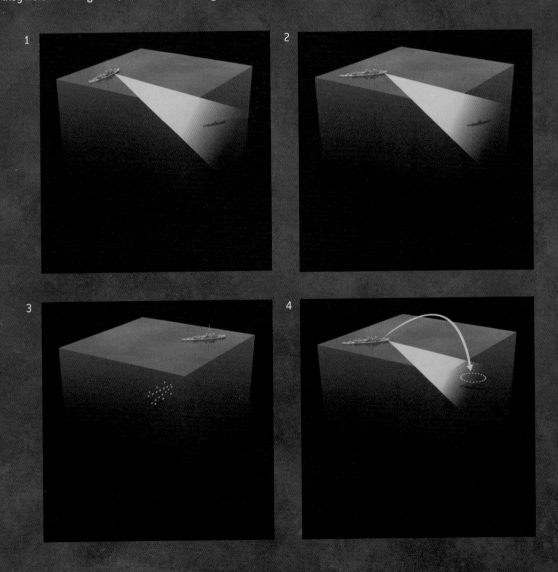

TECHNICAL SPECIFICATIONS

US DESTROYERS AND DESTROYER ESCORTS

The US destroyers and their companion destroyer escorts were finely balanced designs. Everything fit into a hull 290–360ft long and 1,250–2,300 tons displacement, but the optimal mix of these factors for the desired mission required compromise. The Atlantic mission was ASW, rather than the anti-aircraft and anti-ship role needed in the Pacific.

The destroyers assigned to the Atlantic were smaller, older designs, except for the new destroyer escorts, designed specifically for ASW. Both were better suited for use against U-boats than Japanese aircraft or other destroyers. This often meant retrofitting systems, requiring changes in weaponry and propulsion to permit growth in ASW weapons and electronics.

STRUCTURE

The US destroyers were long, lean ships, with length-to-breadth ratios of or exceeding 10:1. The slightly tubbier destroyer escorts, the same width but shorter, had length-to-breadth ratios of 8:1–9:1. Both were packed: engines, boilers, auxiliary machinery, magazines, and fuel tanks filled the hull. Weapons of all sorts covered decks and superstructure.

The two opponents side by side. *U-505*, a Type IXC U-boat, was photographed next to the Edsall-class destroyer escort USS *Pillsbury* (DE-133) shortly after being captured on June 4, 1944 by TG 22.3. *Pillsbury's* crew boarded and captured *U-505*. (USNHHC)

This had two effects. The first was that a hit with a bomb, shell, or torpedo on these vessels would damage something important. The second was more important to the pre-war-design destroyers used in the Atlantic than to the wartime-construction destroyer escorts. Because there was no spare space, any upgrades to weapons, addition of electronics like radar or HF/DF, or improvements such as adding a combat information center (CIC) had to be crammed in. This made a crowded ship even more crowded. In some destroyers the CIC took up part of the officers' wardroom. Adding equipment inevitably increased crew size, further crowding the ship.

There were limits to what could be added, however, especially if topside weight increased enough to threaten stability. Many 1930s-designed US destroyers were "tender," i.e. they were top-heavy enough to risk capsizing when low on fuel. Depth-charge throwers, radar and HF/DF sets and antennae, and additional anti-aircraft weapons raised the ship's center of gravity still further, increasing instability.

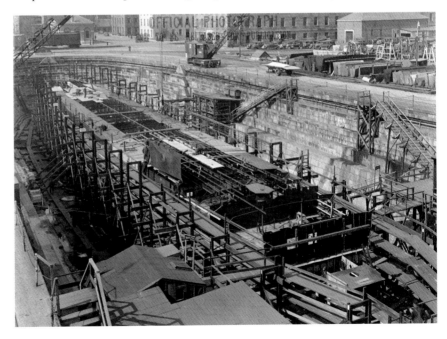

Destroyers were complex structures filled with equipment in a long, lean hull. This can be seen in this photograph of Bagley-class USS *Ralph Talbot* (DD-390), under construction in a drydock at Boston Navy Yard in 1936. (USNHHC)

Reducing top-weight moved the center of gravity back down and involved removing heavy, less critical systems. Obvious candidates were the large, heavy, and high torpedo tubes. Benson- and Gleaves-class destroyers – and sometimes destroyer escorts – lost one set of torpedo tubes because there was no need for ten-torpedo spreads in the Atlantic. Firing even one torpedo occurred only rarely. Boat cranes were also removed, as were most ships' boats. In some destroyers one main gun turret was removed. A 20–25 percent reduction of the main battery was considered an acceptable trade-off for radar, K-gun depth-charge launchers, and additional anti-aircraft weapons.

PROPULSION

High-pressure turbines fed by steam boilers were used to achieve the speeds desired for destroyers. Turbines produced more power at a lower volume and weight than any other marine propulsion system through the middle of the twentieth century. Mechanical efficiency improved with higher steam pressure and temperature, and the US Navy refined their steam plants throughout this period. Flush-deck destroyers' steam engines operated at 300psi, with saturated steam at 420°F (215°C). The Gleaves-class destroyers' steam plants were built to operate at 600psi pressure superheated to 850°F (454°C). The difference was a big reason why Gleaves-class destroyers had nearly double the horsepower of flush-deck destroyers. It also explained why, despite being 30 percent larger than the flush-deckers, they were 1kn faster.

US Navy destroyers were built with two firerooms and two engine rooms. The firerooms contained two boilers each; the engine rooms had one steam engine each. The rooms were compartmentalized so that losing one compartment would not leave the vessel powerless. Up until 1938, the engine rooms were aft of the firerooms to reduce the length of the propeller shafts.

Beginning with the Benson class in 1938, US Navy destroyers alternated boiler rooms and engine rooms. This echeloned arrangement ensured at least one fireroom and one

Although some US Navy destroyer escorts had diesel engines, all US Navy destroyers and one-third of destroyer escorts were powered by steam turbines. This photograph shows the engine-room controls in a destroyer as a water tender conducts throttle watch. (AC)

engine room would be available if any two adjacent compartments were flooded, significantly improving survivability. This arrangement was repeated in subsequent destroyer classes and in steam-powered destroyer escorts. Additionally, starting with the Porter class, built in 1936, all US Navy destroyers had auxiliary diesel generators, which provided electricity (and ran pumps) even if both engines were knocked out.

Two bottlenecks slowed increased destroyer construction: high-performance steam turbines and reduction gearing shortages. Making reduction gears required high-precision machinery that was difficult to build. Destroyer-escort designs attempted to sidestep the shortages by substituting diesel engines for steam plants; a decision that also eliminated complicated boilers.

Several US manufacturers were producing highly reliable 1,500hp diesels, eight of which produced 12,000hp – enough to propel a destroyer escort at 24kn; fast enough, although slower than a destroyer. However, diesels were in demand for US Navy submarines, landing ships, and other small warships. Four 1,500hp diesels produced 6,000hp, yielding a 21kn maximum speed, again fast enough to hunt U-boats. The space for the missing diesels was used for storage. To eliminate reduction gears, the diesels drove generators which powered two electric motors connected to the propellers.

It turned out there were still too few diesels for the desired number of destroyer escorts; but General Electric had a small turbine design providing 6,750hp which could be manufactured in parallel with the larger steam turbines needed for destroyers. Two yielded 13,500hp, which propelled the destroyer escorts at the originally desired 24kn. Most of these also were electric-drive ships, although the last class of steam-powered destroyer escorts used geared turbines. By 1944 reduction gearing was becoming available.

WEAPONRY

US Navy destroyers and destroyer escorts used two sets of weapons to fight U-boats: underwater weapons (depth charges and projectiles launched by Hedgehog or Mousetrap projectors against submerged U-boats) and surface weapons (guns and torpedoes) once U-boats surfaced.

The primary underwater weapon was the depth charge, a cylinder filled with explosive and fitted with a hydrostatic fuse, which detonated the depth charge at a preset depth. Depth charges had been around since World War I and were highly reliable. US Navy destroyers and destroyer escorts used four different types of depth charges against U-boats: the pre-war Mark 6 and Mark 7, and the Mark 8 and Mark 9, which were introduced in 1943.

The Mark 6 had a total weight of 420lb, with a 300lb TNT explosive charge. It had a sink rate of 8ft/sec. The more powerful Mark 7 weighed 745lb, was filled with 600lb of TNT, and sank at 9ft/sec. In 1941 both could be set to explode at depths of 50–300ft. This was too shallow to damage deep U-boats, so by August 1942 the Mark 6 and Mark 7 were fitted with fuses with a maximum depth setting of 600ft. The Mark 6 could be fired from K-gun projectors, while the heavier Mark 7 was typically rolled off depth-charge racks.

The Mark 8 was an "improved" depth charge. It weighed 525lb, with a 270lb TNT charge, and had a sink rate of 11.5ft/sec. It was fitted with a magnetic pistol that

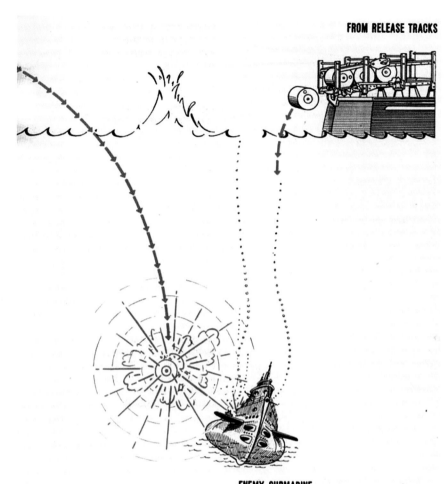

FROM RELEASE TRACKS

ENEMY SUBMARINE

A diagram from a US Navy depth charge ordnance manual showing how depth charges worked. The exploding depth charge was projected from a K-gun, while the other depth charge has been rolled off a depth-charge rack. (AC)

proved unreliable. The Mark 8 also had maintenance issues and was never issued in large numbers. The Mark 9 was more successful. It had a total weight of 320lb, with 200lb of Torpex, and a sink rate of 22.7ft/sec, achieved by its teardrop shape and fins, the latter of which spin-stabilized the depth charge as it sank. Both the Mark 8 and Mark 9 were fitted with hydrostatic pistols which could be set to depths up to 600ft. Later Mark 9s could be set to explode at 1,000ft depth.

In late 1942 the US Navy began introducing forward-firing projectors on ships. These fired 65lb projectiles carrying 35lb of Torpex and with a sink rate of 23.5ft/sec. These projectiles were contact-fused, which meant they dropped until they hit something – a U-boat or the ocean bottom – and exploded on contact. Two types of projectors were used: Hedgehog and Mousetrap. Hedgehog was a steerable platform carrying 24 projectiles launched by spigot mortars. It fired a circular ring of projectiles 267yd across and could be reloaded (six reloads were carried) in three minutes. One hit would sink a U-boat. A single Hedgehog mount was standard on destroyer escorts, but pre-war destroyers had to be retrofitted with a Hedgehog, and often lost one bow gun to make room for it. Mousetrap, which had four or eight rails, launched projectiles using rockets. It had a smaller footprint and less recoil than the Hedgehog projector

31

US NAVY DEPTH CHARGE AND HEDGEHOG PROJECTILE

The standard depth charges used by the US Navy were the Mark 6, 7, and 9. A Mark 8 was developed, but never deployed. The Mark 6 and 7 were improved versions of the Mark 3 and 4 used in World War I. The redesign simplified construction, which made both easier and cheaper to build. The Mark 6 had a total weight of 420lb with 300lb of TNT as the explosive. It had a sink rate of 8ft/sec (2.4m/sec). The Mark 7 was essentially a Mark 6 with a larger diameter (24.875–27.625in). It had a total weight of 745lb with 600lb of TNT and a sink rate of 9ft/sec (2.7m/sec). Both were designed in 1937 and introduced into service in 1938. Through 1942, the Mark 6 and 7 could each be set to explode at any depth between 50 and 300ft. Unfortunately, U-boats routinely dived to 230m (750ft). In August 1942, a new modification allowed both to be set to depths up to 600ft. The main difference between the two was the Mark 7 was too heavy to be launched from K-gun or Y-gun projectors and could only be used from stern racks. The Mark 9, which entered service in 1943, had a streamlined "teardrop" shape with stern-mounted fins imparting a stabilizing spin as it sank. This gave the Mark 9 a much higher sink rate: 22.7ft/sec (6.9m/sec). It had a total weight of 380lb, 200lb of which was the Torpex warhead. It could be set to explode at depths up to 600ft and late-war versions could be set for 1,000ft. The Hedgehog was 46.5in long and had a diameter of 7.2in. It weighed 65lb with a 35lb Torpex warhead. A single hit would sink a U-boat.

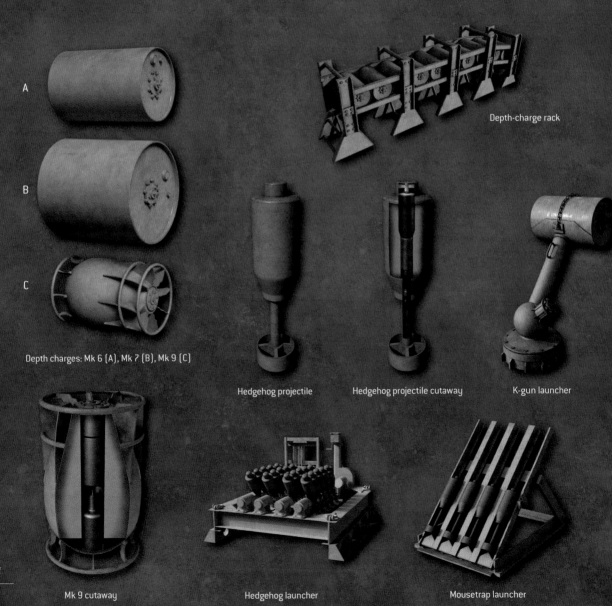

A

B

C

Depth-charge rack

Depth charges: Mk 6 (A), Mk 7 (B), Mk 9 (C)

Hedgehog projectile

Hedgehog projectile cutaway

K-gun launcher

Mk 9 cutaway

Hedgehog launcher

Mousetrap launcher

and was intended for use on smaller ASW vessels. Twelve destroyers were fitted with Mousetraps, because the projectors could be mounted on the sides of the ships.

US Navy destroyers and destroyer escorts involved in the Battle of the Atlantic had a main battery of two to six 3–5in guns, which fired a 24–55lb projectile, easily capable of penetrating a U-boat's pressure hull. They also carried a wide range of anti-aircraft guns ranging from single-mount 0.50in machine guns to quad 40mm Bofors. The Bofors and the 20mm Oerlikon gun mounted on US Navy warships were capable of penetrating a U-boat hull with a well-placed shot. Their main use, however, was to smother a U-boat with anti-personnel fire to prevent the U-boat's crewmen from manning the deck guns.

Both destroyers and destroyer escorts had torpedo tubes. While these were intended for use against surface warships, destroyers occasionally fired a torpedo at a surfaced U-boat if the opportunity arose.

ELECTRONICS

World War II was the first naval war in which electronics – remote sensing and electronic countermeasures – played a critical role. Sonar, radar, radio-direction-finding, and electronic message decryption were key elements of the Allied victory in the Battle of the Atlantic. US Navy destroyers began the war with just sonar, but they and the destroyer escorts which joined them had radar and HF/DF added to their weaponry by the war's end. Most were so equipped by 1943. They also benefited from improvements in sonar and radar technology. Improved sonar and radar were installed throughout the war.

The US Navy had used sonar since the early 1920s. Active sonar projects an acoustical pulse of sound into water, capturing echoes yielding bearing. Range is determined by timing each echo's return. Passive sonar detects sonar pulses, yielding

The 3in/50 dual-purpose gun was the weapon most commonly used by US Navy destroyers and destroyer escorts fighting U-boats. Twenty-seven flush-deck destroyers replaced their original 4in battery with 3in/50s, while four of six destroyer-escort classes had three 3in/50s. (AC)

"HUFF-DUFF"

One of the most ignored tools of the Battle of the Atlantic was High-Frequency Direction Finding (HF/DF or "Huff-Duff"). Shore-based radio direction finders had been locating the approximate positions of U-boats since the beginning of World War II. This permitted defensive use of HF/DF, to route convoys away from known concentrations of U-boats. Later, when combined with signal decryption, HF/DF detections allowed the US Navy to send hunter-killer groups to areas patrolled by U-boats.

Shortly after the United States' entry into the war the Allied navies began installing HF/DF on warships, especially destroyers. This allowed more precise location of U-boats, precise enough that HF/DF could be used tactically. A single HF/DF-equipped destroyer could run down the HF/DF bearing until a U-boat appeared on its radar or sonar. A pair of warships could triangulate the U-boat's position and direct a warship or aircraft to the spot. HF/DF was also the longest-ranged sensor aboard US Navy escort warships, because it could see over the horizon. It was so valuable that in the Atlantic, with its low air threat, air-search radars were removed from warships to permit installation of HF/DF antennae.

The Edsall-class destroyer escort USS *Martin H. Ray* (DE-338) showing its HF/DF antenna (circled). (USNHHC)

only bearing. The first US Navy sonars were tested in 1927. By 1934, QC sonar was being installed on new-construction destroyers. By September 1939, 60 destroyers had sonar installed. By the time the US Navy established the Neutrality Patrol in 1941, that figure had increased to 100, but it was not until mid-1942 that all US Navy destroyers had sonar installed.

QC was a searchlight-style sensor that sent signals on a narrow (14-degree) cone. Another limitation was the rubber dome enclosing the sonar head, which limited destroyer speed to 15kn or less. A steel dome developed by Britain's Royal Navy and shared with the US increased search speeds to 20–24kn. Installation of the steel dome on US Navy destroyers began in November 1941. Sonar worked best when a submarine's bearing was known. Over time, operator skill improved efficiency significantly, so that by 1943 enough proficient sonarmen existed to make sonar a highly effective asset.

Radar was the most important addition to the US Navy's electronic arsenal in World War II. It allowed escorts to track U-boats during night or foul weather, stripping U-boats of the anonymity darkness gave them. The US Navy, however, had no destroyers equipped with radar when the Neutrality Patrol began. Even after the United States entered the war, few US Navy destroyers operating in the Atlantic were equipped with surface-search radar. The Wickes-class flush-deck destroyer USS *Roper* (DD-147) may have been the first such vessel so equipped, fitted experimentally with a British radar. Thereafter the US Navy began installing radar on destroyers as soon as they became available. As 1943 began, the retrofitting of existing destroyers with radar was complete and new construction had radar as built – a major reason for an improvement in ASW efficiency. Similarly, new construction was outfitted with HF/DF antennae, providing another means of detecting and tracking U-boats.

GERMAN U-BOATS

US Navy warships primarily fought battles with two German U-boats types: the Type VII and Type IX. (Type II U-boats were withdrawn from the Atlantic before the United States entered the war.) Type X and Type XIV supply U-boats were incapable of fighting, while Type XXI and Type XIII U-boats conducted war patrols outside areas of US Navy responsibility.

The US encountered every Type VII variant (Type VIIA, VIIB, VIIC, VIIC/41, and VIIF) and Type IX variant (Type IX, IXB, IXC, IXC/40, and IXD) that saw combat. Germany began the war with Type VIIA and Type IX U-boats. Type VIIB, VIIC, IXB, IXC, and IXC/40 U-boats were incremental improvements on previous versions, increasing fuel and torpedo storage capacity and marginally increasing speed. The Type VIIC/41 was a 1941 improvement of the Type VIIC with a thicker hull, permitting deeper diving.

STRUCTURE

All German U-boats used a double-hull design. The inner hull was the pressure hull, a steel cylinder with a steel hemisphere at each end. Atop the pressure hull, roughly amidships, was the conning tower, cylindrical with a hemispherical top. The crew lived within the pressure hull and conning tower, and worked in them when the U-boat was submerged.

The pressure hull maintained 1 atmosphere pressure, despite the depth of the U-boat, until the U-boat passed the crush depth, the depth at which water pressure exceeded the ability of the pressure vessel's steel hull to resist it. Then the hull collapsed, crushing its contents. The crush depth was an unknown quantity for each individual U-boat, but it was known to be below the vessel's test depth – the maximum depth an intact U-boat could safely dive. For Type VII and Type IX U-boats the test depth was 230m (750ft), deeper than any other nation's submarines could safely dive.

The pressure hull was pierced by numerous openings. There were four hatches: the forward and aft torpedo hatch, through which torpedoes were loaded; the galley hatch, allowing stores to be taken directly to the galley; and the conning tower hatch, used almost exclusively when the U-boat was at sea. (The other three hatches were on the deck, easily swamped by waves.) There were also torpedo tubes – four in the bow and one (for Type VII U-boats) or two (for Type IX U-boats) in the stern. Finally a multitude of small openings existed, through which cables, pipes,

U-568

U-568 was a Type VIIC, the most widely produced U-boat, with 568 commissioned. They were designed for use in the eastern Atlantic, east of Iceland in the Western Approaches to Britain. They were also intended to operate in concert with other Type VII U-boats using *Rudeltaktik*, attacking convoys in wolf packs of six or more U-boats. Their range was increased by the capture of French Atlantic Coast bases, which allowed them to conduct wolf-pack attacks as far west as Newfoundland, Canada or conduct individual patrols along the North Atlantic coast. *U-568* was commissioned in May 1941, and conducted five war patrols before being sunk. It was best known for torpedoing USS *Kearny* in October 1941.

U-boats had a sturdy, cylindrical pressure hull which maintained the crew at a 1 atmosphere pressure even at test depth despite the multiple openings cut into the pressure hull (seen in this bow view of a U-boat under construction). (AC)

and control shafts penetrated. All had to be sealed before the U-boat dived and strong enough to resist water pressure at depth to prevent leaking. Damage limited the depth that could safely be reached, as higher water pressure at lower depths triggered leaks.

The pressure hull was divided in half horizontally along the forward two-thirds of the hull. Below were the bilges and batteries, above was the crew working space. In the aft third of the U-boat the diesel engines and electric motors occupied the entire pressure hull.

Surrounding the pressure hull was the outer casing, forming a hydrodynamic shell around the pressure hull. While the casing streamlined the hull, it was not designed for optimal underwater movement. It was topped by a flat deck on which deck guns were located, along with containers for external stowage of spare torpedoes and other items (including escape life rafts). The bridge superstructure rested on the deck, as did

U-568	
Displacement	769 tons surfaced; 871 tons submerged; 1,070 full load
Dimensions	Length 67.1m (220ft 3in); beam 6.2m (20ft 4in); draft 4.74m (15ft 7in)
Machinery	Two Germaniawerft F46 6-cylinder diesels with 3,200shp driving two shafts; two BBC GG UB 720/8 electric motors with 740shp
Speed	17.7kn surfaced; 7.6kn submerged
Range	8,500nm at 18kn surfaced; 80nm at 4kn submerged
Fuel	Diesel oil
Crew	Four officers, 40–52 men
Armament	Five 533mm (21in) torpedo tubes (four forward, one aft) and 14 533mm (21in) torpedoes; one 88mm/65 deck gun; one 20mm AA gun

U-549	
Displacement	1,120 tons surfaced; 1,232 tons submerged; 1,545 full load
Dimensions	Length 76.76m (251ft 103in); beam 6.86m (22ft 6in); draft 4.67m (15ft 4in)
Machinery	Two MAN M 9 V 40/46 9-cylinder diesels with 4,400shp driving two shafts; two Siemens-Schuckert 2 GU 345/34 electric motors with 1,000shp
Speed	19kn surfaced; 7.3kn submerged
Range	13,850nm at 18kn surfaced; 64nm at 4kn submerged
Fuel	Diesel oil
Crew	Four officers, 44 men
Armament	Six 533mm (21in) torpedo tubes (four forward, two aft) and 22 533mm (21in) torpedoes; one 37mm SK C/30 AA gun; two 20mm flak 30 AA guns (1x2)

platforms for anti-aircraft guns. Fuel and ballast tanks were located on the sides between the two hulls. Ballast tanks could be filled with water or air to allow the U-boat to dive or surface.

PROPULSION

Every U-boat was equipped with two diesel engines. The Type VII had two supercharged six-cylinder, four-stroke engines, but the engine used depended on the U-boat variant. Type VIIA, most VIIB, and a few VIIC U-boats had two MAN six-cylinder, four-stroke M6V 40/46 diesels, each producing 1,050–1,155 brake horsepower. Starting with the Type VIIB U-boat, Germaniawerft six-cylinder,

The G7 torpedo – U-boat crews called them "eels" – one of which is seen being loaded into a U-boat in a German harbor, was a U-boat's most lethal threat. A single hit by a G7 torpedo would sink most merchantmen and cripple or sink a destroyer. (AC)

U-549

U-549 was one of 193 Type IX U-boats commissioned in the Kriegsmarine. It was a Type IXC/40 design, of which 87 were commissioned. All Type IXs were designed as long-range U-boats, intended to patrol individually in distant waters where there were no convoys. The Type IXC/40 was a very long-range version. It could travel 13,850nm without refueling (only the Type IXD had a longer range). This plate depicts *U-549* as it appeared during its second war patrol.

four-stroke F46 diesels were installed, each producing 1,400–1,600hp. The Type IX U-boats were equipped with two MAN 40/46 supercharged nine-cylinder, four-stroke diesels, each producing 2,200hp.

U-boats were also fitted with two electric motors. Early Type VII, all Type VIIA, and around half of the Type VIIB U-boats were outfitted with Brown, Boveri & Cie (BBC) GG UB 720/8 double-acting electric motors, together totalling 750hp. The rest of the Type VIIB, early Type VIIC, and Type VIID U-boats were fitted with AEG GU 460/8-276 electric motors. Later Type VIIs, as well as the Type VIIC/41s, had BBC GG UB 720/8, Garbe, Lahmeyer & Co. RP 137/c, or Siemens-Schuckert-Werke (SSW) GU 343/38-8 electric motors which produced 375hp each. Type IX U-boats had two SSW 500hp GU 345/34 electric motors. All of these motors ran off power stored in banks of batteries in the lower half of the pressure hull forward of the engine room.

Two sets of engines were required to enable prolonged submerged activity. Diesels were more efficient and more powerful than electric motors; but they were internal-combustion engines requiring air to burn fuel, and producing toxic combustion gases that needed to be exhausted. If run while the U-boat was submerged, without access to the surface to draw air and exhaust burnt fuel, they soon asphyxiated the crew. The solution was to run the diesels while surfaced, using them to drive the U-boat's twin propellers through geared connections, and drive a generator to charge the storage batteries.

The diesels were shut down when the U-boat submerged. It was then propelled by the electric motors, drawing electricity from the previously charged batteries. The electric motors could also drive the U-boat when it was surfaced, using the diesels only for the generators; but this was less fuel-efficient – and no competent U-boat skipper wasted fuel.

This worked well, during the early war years, when radar and maritime patrol aircraft were scarce. Submarines ran surfaced to reach their patrol areas with impunity. By 1942, however, radar and aircraft were making running surfaced hazardous during daylight hours and risky at night. By 1943, daylight surfaced operations were almost suicidal and even running surfaced at night was hazardous. To overcome this risk, the Kriegsmarine began equipping U-boats with Schnorchels.

A Schnorchel was a pair of tubes, one for air and one for engine exhaust, which could be raised above the sea's surface when a U-boat was submerged. A stop valve at the top prevented water from entering the tubes when the Schnorchel-head was swamped by waves. With the Schnorchel-head above water, the diesels could run, drawing air from the surface. A "snorting" U-boat, making use of a Schnorchel, provided a minimal radar and visual profile. Only the Schnorchel-head could be spotted by radar. Under some circumstances, the diesels' exhaust plume could be sighted, but this was difficult.

Snorting was inconvenient because a U-boat could dive no deeper than periscope depth. If the Schnorchel-head was swamped, the diesels drew air from within the U-boat until the Schnorchel-head was again above water. The diesels were noisy, preventing hydrophones from being used, and making the U-boat easier to detect by a surface warship's hydrophones. Additionally, submerged U-boats were detectable by sonar. The combination made it easier for a warship to detect a U-boat and then attack it undetected.

WEAPONRY

The U-boat's primary weapon against a destroyer or destroyer escort was its 533mm (21in) torpedoes. Although U-boats carried deck guns, a gunnery duel with a destroyer was a mismatch. Not only did the warship's main battery outnumber the U-boat's deck guns, the destroyers had a large suite of anti-aircraft guns, effective in supressing any U-boat gun crews. By 1942, U-boats were having their deck guns removed to allow more anti-aircraft guns – useful against attacking aircraft – to be carried.

When the US Navy began fighting U-boats in fall 1941, the two main torpedoes in service were the G7a T1 compressed-air torpedo and the G7e T2 electrically powered torpedo. Both carried a 280kg (617lb) Hexanite-filled warhead and contact triggers, which detonated upon striking a ship. More powerful than TNT, a single hit by a Hexanite-filled warhead could cripple or sink a US Navy destroyer.

Both the G7a and G7e torpedoes were also fitted with Federapparattorpedo (FAT; spring-operated torpedo) gearing during 1941 or Lagenunabhängiger Torpedo (LUT; a more sophisticated version of FAT) gearing after mid-1944. Both permitted a torpedo to zigzag back and forth after traveling straight for a preset distance. They were effective against convoys, but generally of little use in stopping a destroyer intent on attacking a U-boat. The un-aimed looping torpedo was easily evaded once a destroyer was aware of its presence.

The G7a torpedo had a range of 8,000m (8,749yd) when set for 40kn or 14,000m (15,311yd) at 30kn. It left a visible surface trail of bubbles as it traveled, potentially alerting targets of their approach. The G7e torpedo could reach 5,000m (5,468yd) at its 30kn setting, if preheated. The G7e left no trail of bubbles and was simpler to manufacture.

In 1943, Germany introduced an acoustic torpedo that they called *Zaunkönig* (Wren) and the Allies the German Naval Acoustic Torpedo (GNAT). This torpedo homed in on the target's propeller noise. To prevent it from running in a circle and hitting the U-boat that launched it, the torpedo followed an initial straight course for 731.5m (800yd) and had to be fired from a depth of at

Every U-boat was powered by two diesel engines: six-cylinder engines on Type VII U-boats, or (as show here) nine-cylinder engines on Type IX U-boats. This photo was taken through the engine-room hatch. (AC)

GERMAN TORPEDOES

U-boats used three basic types of torpedo during World War II, all variants on the Kaiserliche Marine's World War I G7 torpedo. They were the (A) G7a T1 Ato, (B) G7e T2 and T3 Eto, and (C) G7e T5 *Zaunkönig*. Ato was steam powered, Eto electric powered, and *Zaunkönig* was an electric torpedo fitted with an acoustic warhead. Ato was the oldest, developed in 1930 and entering service in 1938. It burned decalin with hydrogen peroxide to generate steam, driving counter-rotating propellers. It was highly reliable and could drive a torpedo 6,000m (6,560yd) at 44kn, 8,000m (8,750yd) at 40kn, or 14,000m (15,310yd) at 30kn. A trail of bubbles marked its wake. Eto entered service in 1939. It used wet-cell batteries to run an electric motor. It had a shorter range: 5,000m (5,470yd) at 30kn for early-war versions and 7,500m (8,200yd) at 30kn later in the war. It achieved those speeds and ranges only if preheated to 30°C. It was wakeless, allowing undetected attacks. *Zaunkönig* (shown in cutaway) was an Eto with a new warhead. An acoustic tracker sensed noise at 24.5kHz (produced by propeller cavitation from an escort warship traveling at 10–18kn). This was connected to steering that aimed the torpedo at the source of the noise. The *Zaunkönig* had a range of 5,700m (6,230yd) at 24–25kn. Some 700 *Zaunkönigs* were fired by U-boats, sinking 77 ships.

All three were 7.186m (23ft 7in) long with an exterior diameter of 533mm (21in) and weight of 1,500–1,605kg (3,307–3,538lb). Ato and Eto each had a 280kg (617lb) Hexanite-filled warhead. The *Zaunkönig* had a 200kg (441lb) warhead due to the size of the acoustic tracker.

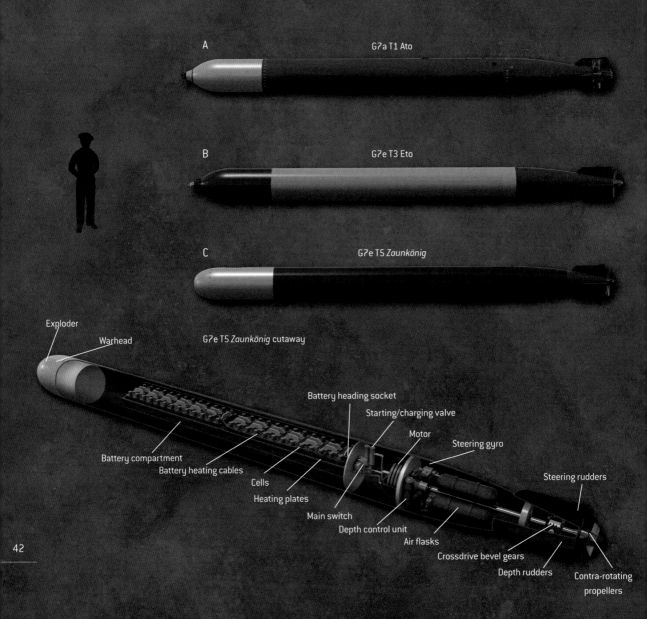

A   G7a T1 Ato

B   G7e T3 Eto

C   G7e T5 *Zaunkönig*

G7e T5 *Zaunkönig* cutaway

Exploder

Warhead

Battery heading socket

Starting/charging valve

Motor

Steering gyro

Battery compartment

Battery heating cables

Cells

Heating plates

Main switch

Depth control unit

Air flasks

Crossdrive bevel gears

Depth rudders

Steering rudders

Contra-rotating propellers

least 30.5m (100ft). It had a 24kn speed and a 6,000m (6,562yd) range. Intended for use against escort warships, it was initially highly successful, but countermeasures developed prior to its August 1943 introduction were deployed soon after, and its effectiveness dropped dramatically thereafter.

ELECTRONICS

The Allies' increasing use of radar led to German countermeasures. The first was the Metox radar detector, a collapsible, five-piece wooden-frame antenna mounted on the conning tower when the U-boat surfaced. Metox picked up emissions broadcast from meter-wave radar, both airborne and ship-mounted. The receiver beeped when it detected radar signals, the beeping increasing if the U-boat were detected. Introduced in August 1942, Metox proved effective until April 1943, when the Allies introduced centimeter-wave radars operating on wavelengths undetectable to Metox. German intelligence began to believe the Allies were using Metox to home in on U-boats. As a consequence, in August 1943 U-boats were instructed to discontinue using Metox, and it was retired from service.

Metox was followed by Naxos, a radar detector capturing centimeter-wave transmissions. Telefunken of Germany manufactured the detector, and it was introduced into Kriegsmarine service September 1943. Deployment was delayed due to fears the Allies could track U-boats from Naxos, but by December 1943, it was being installed on U-boats. By then, however, the Allies were introducing radars invisible to Naxos.

Two types of search radar were eventually installed in U-boats: FuMO 61 Hohentwiel-U and FuMO 63, Hohentwiel-K. They had a search range of 8–19km (5–12 miles), hardly beyond daytime visual range. Additionally, the Kriegsmarine vastly overestimated the effectiveness of passive radar. The result was most skippers commanding U-boats equipped with radar kept their radar sets switched off, to prevent passive detection that was not happening.

The Kriegsmarine became aware the Allies were using radio direction-finding to fix the locations of transmitting U-boats, and equally aware of its high effectiveness. To counter this it developed Kurier, a burst-transmission system. Kurier compressed coded messages from a 20-second transmission time to a 0.25-second burst – too short for effective direction-finding. Sea trials were conducted in 1943, but installation lagged and Kurier did not reach operational U-boats until the second half of 1944.

Kurier also protected U-boats from Allied codebreaking. The Allies had been reading German transmissions coded with the Enigma cipher machine since early 1943. Despite having had its codes cracked in World War I, Germany ignored the threat in World War II. Frequently, Kurier burst transmissions were not intercepted and decoded, their benefit downgraded because messages to U-boats were sent conventionally and continued to be read.

A major handicap for U-boats was their limited electronics. Radar was installed late and used reluctantly. Even radar detectors were believed to be problematic. U-boats largely relied on visual detection to find targets, hence this sailor on lookout duty in the tropics. (AC)

43

THE COMBATANTS

The prospect of free travel was one reason many men joined the US Navy or the Kriegsmarine. They promised, "Join the navy and see the world." Throwing in technical training created a preference for naval service over the US Army. (USNHHC)

The combatants came from two navies with significant similarities and significant differences. Both were all-volunteer forces: neither the US Navy nor the Kriegsmarine conscripted personnel. Before each nation entered the war, service in both navies was strictly voluntary. Each navy could afford to be picky when enlisting men. Even after the war began, neither navy impressed or drafted personnel. However, some men volunteered for their nation's navy to avoid being conscripted into the army. Regardless, both navies maintained higher personnel standards than did their respective armies.

One major difference between the two navies was the size of growth. The Kriegsmarine began World War II in September 1939 with 78,000 men and grew to a maximum strength of 810,000 in 1944. The US Navy had 126,418 men in September 1939 and grew to 3.2 million personnel by the end of 1944. While the Kriegsmarine had ten men in 1944 for every one it had in 1939, the US Navy had over 25.

An additional difference was that the US Navy had national leadership that understood its navy and supported it. The Kriegsmarine did not. President Roosevelt had been a yachtsman and served as Assistant Secretary of the Navy in 1913–20. Adolph Hitler never understood sea power, and mistrusted the Kriegsmarine's leadership until Dönitz took over in 1943.

JOIN THE NAVY

AND SEE THE WORLD

THE UNITED STATES NAVY SAILOR

The United States Navy dated to 1794 when the United States Congress authorized the creation of a navy to replace the Continental Navy established in 1776 and disbanded in 1785. Between 1794 and 1939 the US Navy remained a relatively small, highly professional service with a history of winning small, short wars with existing ships and personnel and an ability to expand rapidly during major conflicts. World War II marked a period of unprecedented growth in the US Navy and a period when it gained the ability to project power throughout the world.

During the 1920s and 1930s the US Navy relied on highly professional long-service sailors in both enlisted and officer ranks. Especially during the Depression years of the 1930s, when civilian jobs were scarce, the Navy was highly selective of those permitted to serve, allowing only the best to re-enlist.

This changed only with the start of World War II in September 1939. Although the United States was neutral through December 1941, it anticipated entry into the war. It began preparations to expand the Navy in the late 1930s, including vastly expanded numbers of both enlisted and commissioned personnel. Despite rapid expansion, however, enlistment remained voluntary through the first year of the war. Growth of the Navy was such that on February 1, 1943 it ended voluntary enlistment of men aged 18–37 inclusive, and turned to conscription to fill its ranks; but even with that, 60 percent of those who served in the Navy during World War II, including all officers, were volunteers.

The US Navy had higher physical and mental standards for enlistment than the US Army prior to and through January 1943. The higher standards were needed as the US Navy was a highly technical service in the mid-twentieth century. Many preferred naval service due to better living conditions and the opportunity to learn skills that would be transferrable to peacetime employment. However, conscription was run by the Selective Service System, which procured men for both the Navy and the Army. Thereafter, Army standards were used for recruits of both services.

The pre-war officers and men served as a cadre for the wartime US Navy with its reserve officers and wartime enlistees. Some regular officers and veteran sailors served in the forces that fought the Battle of the Atlantic. However, most experienced personnel were drawn to larger warships. The destroyers and destroyer escorts that fought the U-boats were largely manned by reservist officers and wartime recruits, especially after June 1942.

Training was a continuous process in the US Navy. It began when an individual entered the service, and ended when he left it. All men enlisting in the US Navy began their careers at Navy Boot Camp. (Until Women Accepted for Volunteer Emergency Service – WAVES – was organized in July 1942, the US Navy was all-male. Even

A young US Navy boot recruit grinning broadly during training. For many young "boots," training camp was the first time away from home, and the adventure of a lifetime. (AC)

45

after that, WAVES was limited to shore assignments and did not serve aboard warships.)

Prior to World War II there were four Navy Boot Camps: San Diego, California; Bainbridge, Maryland; Newport, Rhode Island; and Great Lakes, Illinois. Three more were added during World War II: Norfolk, Virginia; Sampson, New York; and Farragut, Idaho. Boot Camp normally lasted six weeks. During World War II, depending on the needs of the service for personnel, it could be shortened to as little as four weeks or lengthened to eight weeks. At Boot Camp, recruits were issued their uniform and kit (including a copy of the *Bluejackets' Manual*) and learned the fundamentals of being a sailor: basic drill, seamanship, naval customs and courtesy, small-arms training, swimming, and how to live aboard ship.

Upon graduation, the new seamen were either assigned directly to ships, where they learned their duties through what was essentially an apprenticeship, or were assigned to a school where they received specialty training. There were three categories of schools. Class-A schools provided elementary instruction to recruits in technical fields and gave them the groundwork necessary to move into the lowest petty-officer ratings. These technical fields included a broad range of specialties – electrical, ordnance, communications, clerical, machinists, metalworkers, woodworkers, radiomen, diesel-engine mechanics, hospital corpsmen, even bugling.

Class-B schools gave enlisted men more advanced instruction. This included courses in advanced machinery such as bombsights, optics, or gyrocompasses, firefighting, or torpedoman training. Typically, men attending those schools had some experience in the US Navy, and were not raw recruits. Class-C schools were more advanced still, providing training in subjects not normally part of shipboard instruction. Men accepted into these schools were either in the top part of their recruit class for Class-A schools or had demonstrated superior capability during service at sea.

Although it sounded rickety, the system worked well. While operating a ship required many specialized skills, it also required much unskilled labor. The US Navy had a long tradition of on-the-job training, with sailors "striking" (training for) more skilled positions than their current assignment while at sea. Recruits did necessary unskilled work upon arriving at their ships, at the guns, in the machinery rooms, or as part of the deck crew. They learned additional skills as they spent time on board their ship.

In World War II the US Navy was rigidly segregated. While Hispanic and Native Americans were largely treated as "white" for service purposes, before and during the war's opening years, black and Asian Americans (especially those who were Chinese or Filipino) could only serve as messmen or stewards. This changed in June 1942, when African-American soldiers were permitted to enlist for general service. While the US Navy remained the US Armed Forces' most segregated service, by the end of World War II some warships, generally destroyer escorts such as the Evarts-class USS *Mason* (DE-529), were being manned by black enlisted men with white officers, and black men were being accepted as officers.

At sea responsibility came calling with every four-hour watch. This young man scans the horizon in foul weather seeking any glimpse of the enemy. In the Atlantic, it might be no more than the trail of a U-boat's raised periscope. (AC)

Black men were not allowed to serve in any position other than as cooks or mess boys when the US Navy entered World War II. By 1943 they could serve in combat roles, such as this 20mm gun crew. One destroyer escort in the Atlantic, the Evarts-class USS *Mason* (DE-529), had a largely African-American crew. (AC)

The US Navy's officers were largely long-serving, professional officers prior to World War II. Most were graduates of the United States Naval Academy at Annapolis, Maryland, who had gone through a four-year training period, including a college education and summer cruises. Officers were expected to be gentlemen as well as mariners, which meant they were expected to have a college education, and to serve as leaders.

With the growth in the size of the fleet, which began in 1935, the US Navy realized this officer corps was too small for the intended expansion. It therefore initiated a Reserve Officer Training Corps (ROTC) system at American colleges and universities, whereby students received naval training along with their baccalaureate degrees, gaining a reserve commission upon graduation. This included men attending maritime academies receiving training to serve as merchant marine officers.

During World War II, ROTC training was vastly expanded, including the creation of the V-7 program in June 1940 and the V-12 program in July 1943. V-7 candidates attended college, went through an eight-month United States Naval Reserve Midshipmen's School, and received an ensign's commission upon graduation. V-12 midshipmen attended civilian colleges, supplementing that education with roughly 12 months' training to become a naval officer.

The V-7 program was intended to create 36,000 officers, while the V-12 program had a target of 200,000 officers. By the time World War II ended, these two programs had created 97,000 officers. (Another 131,000 officers were appointed directly from civilian life, including many with pre-war college degrees who went through Reserve Officer training. In some cases these men received rapid promotion based on their existing experience and skills.)

The men who served aboard US Navy destroyers and destroyer escorts fighting the U-boats in the Atlantic were generally younger and more athletic than those assigned to larger warships. Destroyers and destroyer escorts were small warships, tossed about during rough weather, and they were cramped. Regulars, both enlisted and commissioned, largely manned the anti-submarine forces in the second half of 1941, during the months of the Neutrality Patrol, and into the first months of 1942. However these men were needed in the Pacific, to fight the massive naval war with Japan, and they were soon drawn west, their ranks replaced by recruits and reserves.

By 1943, regulars were commanding destroyers with one or two Annapolis men in the wardroom, but by the following year, reserve officers were taking command of ASW warships. Annapolis men remained in command of task and escort groups, with a few junior regulars in charge of destroyers and destroyer escorts. Reserves filled the remaining slots. Similarly, enlisted men who served as seamen first class in 1939 and 1940 had moved up. A few of these regulars leavened the enlisted ranks in the warships battling the U-boats. The most capable had become petty officers or chief petty officers. Despite the vast expansion of the US Navy, destroyermen serving in the Atlantic remained a capable and competent force.

THE KRIEGSMARINE *U-BOOTSMANN*

The men and officers who served aboard Germany's U-boats were members of the Kriegsmarine (War Navy), which was created in 1935. Its origins dated to the creation of the Kaiserliche Marine (Imperial German Navy), formed in 1871. With Germany's defeat in World War I the Kaiserliche Marine became the Reichsmarine (Realm Navy) in 1919, before being re-named the Kriegsmarine two years after Hitler took power in 1933. Yet it was essentially the same organization. Many Kriegsmarine senior officers started in the Kaiserliche Marine and were combat veterans of World War I.

When World War II began, the Kriegsmarine was an all-volunteer service. Its manpower demands remained small throughout the war when compared to those of the Wehrmacht (Armed Forces) as a whole, allowing it to remain an all-volunteer service

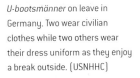

U-bootsmänner on leave in Germany. Two wear civilian clothes while two others wear their dress uniform as they enjoy a break outside. (USNHHC)

until the war ended. The Kriegsmarine's size meant it could be picky about those whom it enlisted. High German pre-war unemployment levels and men preferring naval service to the Heer (Army) during the war ensured a surplus of applicants. (During the war, malefactors could be transferred to the Heer – a prospect that encouraged good behavior.)

Recruits joined the Kriegsmarine when they were aged 17–23. Those younger than 21 needed parental permission to join. All recruits had to be physically fit, in good health (including having good teeth), and of at least average intelligence. They also had to prove that they had completed secondary education and were of German nationality. A criminal record prevented enlistment. Applicants were drawn from all over Germany, both inland and coastal regions. Those who served in Germany's merchant fleet or possessed appropriate technical skills (including having completed apprenticeships) in mechanics and electricity were preferred.

Recruits joined for at least five years, the first of which was given over to training and becoming *Matrosen* (sailors). Once in the Kriegsmarine, recruits were assigned to one of 12 specialties, which ranged from seaman to coastal artilleryman. Half were assigned as seamen. Others specialized in skills needed in the engine rooms, to man the helm, operate the weapons, or administer paperwork. A few became medical orderlies or musicians.

Kriegsmarine recruits went through the same basic training as Heer infantry, right down to wearing Heer *feldgrau* (field-gray, a greenish-gray color) uniforms and undertaking infantry drill and weapons training. After completing this training they were passed to specialist training schools in Kiel, Mürwick, and Swinemünde. From there they went to service assignments. Trained recruits were given the rank of *Matrose* (ordinary seaman).

After a year's service, the *Matrose* could expect promotion to *Matrosengefreiter* (able seaman). Long-service men, those with at least five years' service as a *Matrosengefreiter*, could receive promotion to *Matrosenhauptgefreiter* (high able seaman). The rank carried no extra pay or responsibility, but carried extra respect and prestige.

Promotion to *Maat* (petty officer) depended on the recommendation of an officer. Men accepting promotion lengthened their career obligation from four years to 12. During wartime or periods of rapid expansion, promising recruits could be offered an opportunity to become a *Maat* after basic training. Those accepting the promotion

Life aboard a U-boat was crowded. "Hot-bunking" (two men sleeping in the same bunk at alternate hours) was required. These four men enjoy an off-hours card game amid the paraphernalia of their quarters. (AC)

On watch in the control room. Operating a U-boat required a skilled, professional, and dedicated crew. The men aboard the U-boats maintained their skill and professionalism throughout the war, despite the odds against them. (AC)

after completing basic training went to their specialist training first. Every candidate for promotion to *Maat* went to the *Marineunteroffizierlehrabteilung* (petty officer school) at either Friedrichsort or (after 1938) Wesermünde. There they went through leadership and combat training given Heer NCOs, again donning feldgrau uniforms, and going through simulated land combat as part of their training.

After three years as *Maat*, a sailor could receive promotion to *Obermaat* (petty officer 2nd class). Senior enlisted personnel could become warrant officers (the equivalent of senior petty officers in the US Navy and Royal Navy). There were three tracks: one for shore-based personnel, one for deck personnel, and one for navigation specialists. The titles differed for each track. Warrant officers were the backbone of a Kriegsmarine ship. The most senior warrant ranks were given to those considered good enough to retain after they had completed their 12-year service obligation.

Kriegsmarine officers joining after 1919 came from egalitarian backgrounds, and passed through a recruitment process similar to that of the enlisted personnel. Along with demonstrating their German background, officer candidates also had to provide information on their parents and grandparents, to ensure they too were properly German.

Officer training was rigorous. A Kriegsmarine officer was expected to be a competent seaman and navigator as well as a leader. They went through the same basic training as *Matrosen*, followed by four months of practical training, depending on their career specialty. Officers followed one of four career paths: they could be *Offizier zur See* (line officers), *Ingenieur* (engineering officers), *Waffen-offizier* (weapons specialists), or administrative staff.

Upon completion of officer training they were promoted to cadet, serving nine months on a training ship. Eighteen months of advanced training followed for line and engineering candidates (two years for gunnery officers), followed by six months of fleet service. Only then were they promoted to *Leutnant* (lieutenant – equivalent to a Royal Navy or US Navy ensign). From then on the promotion sequence was *Oberleutnant* (Lieutenant J.G.), *Kapitänleutnant* (Lieutenant), *Korvettenkapitän* (Lieutenant-Commander), *Fregattenkapitän* (Commander), and *Kapitän* (Captain). A *Kapitän* commanded heavy cruisers or larger warships.

Officers destined for U-boat service went through a 12-week training course, which alternated classroom training with seagoing exercises, including making 15 successful attacks from training simulators. Upon completion they then went for advanced training at sea which covered U-boat handling, basic tactical theory, torpedo shooting, and tactical training.

Both men and officers entered U-boat service after completing training. For enlisted personnel this was after they completed their specialized training. For officers it was after they completed advanced training. Officers and men serving aboard surface ships (or ashore) went directly to active-service assignments. Those volunteering for (or being transferred to) submarine duty attended a school to prepare for service in U-boats, initially the Unterseebootsabwehrschule (U-boat fighting school) in Kiel. (The name was intentionally ambiguous to conceal the fact it was a school dedicated not to fighting submarines but rather to how to fight *with* them.)

By 1938 this had evolved into a flotilla of U-boats used exclusively for training. These were stationed at Neustadt in Holstein. During World War II the U-boat training bases were expanded and all training was conducted in the Baltic Sea.

Prior to the war, crews spent up to six months on training U-boats before being assigned to an operational U-boat. Even after the war began, the lack of available operational U-boats allowed the Kriegsmarine the luxury of maintaining this leisurely training schedule. This changed in 1942, when enough U-boats became available that training schedules were shortened to expand the operational fleet. Much of the training done in the training flotillas was transferred to the working-up of new construction.

When a U-boat neared completion a crew was assembled for the vessel. Prior to launch the captain and senior crew member assigned to the U-boat were sent to the relevant shipyard, where they familiarized themselves with the vessel and saw it through completion. In the last weeks before launch they were joined by the rest of the crew, a mixture of veteran U-boat men and newly trained personnel.

After launch and completion the U-boat and its crew went through acceptance testing, including diving trials, silent-running tests, and a general "shakedown" of the U-boat's equipment and machinery. This typically took three weeks.

Technical training for combat followed, comprised of a rigorous set of exercises to prepare the U-boat for active service. It included deep-dive tests and realistic combat exercises. Combat veterans would ride aboard during these exercises and declare unexpected failures to test the captain's reaction. This was intensive training with sometimes deadly results – 30 U-boats were lost during training.

Initially, service in the U-boat force was all-volunteer. This made the force an elite in the pre-war and early-war years. The explosive expansion of U-boat service changed this. By 1942, men were being assigned to the U-boat service without volunteering. However, since the Kriegsmarine was an all-volunteer service, this had less of an impact on morale and competence than is commonly thought.

The large majority of U-boat crewmen were patriotic Germans, and the crews were still professionals. Furthermore, in a U-boat more than any other vessel, individual survival depended on the competence of every crewman. If a U-boat was sunk, more often than not everyone aboard died. Survival motivated performance. As a result, the U-boat force started out with high morale and managed to maintain it throughout the war. The crews continued to go out and fight throughout the war, even at the end when they knew the odds were against them, if not for the Führer then for their country and most of all for their comrades aboard their U-boat.

JESSE CLYBURN SOWELL

Born in Lancaster, South Carolina, on October 16, 1903, Jesse Clyburn Sowell was representative of the US Navy officers who commanded destroyers and destroyer groups during World War II.

He attended the United States Naval Academy in Annapolis from 1921 through 1925 and was commissioned ensign in June 1925. Upon commissioning he served aboard the Omaha-class light cruiser USS *Memphis* (CL-13), flagship of Naval Forces, Europe from then until June 1928. Between 1929 and 1937 he was almost continuously on ship duty, serving respectively in the Clemson-class destroyer USS *McCormick* (DD-223) in the Asiatic Fleet, the river gunboat USS *Luzon* (PR-7), on Yangtze Patrol, the Lapwing-class minesweeper USS *Bittern* (AM-36), in the Asiatic Fleet, the Wickes-class destroyer USS *Montgomery* (DM-21), at San Diego, California, the destroyer tender USS *Melville* (AD-2), and the Farragut-class destroyer USS *Farragut* (DD-348).

Sowell's only break from sea duty was attending the Navy Postgraduate School in Annapolis and receiving instruction at the Naval Boiler Factory in Philadelphia from July 1932 through June 1934. In March 1937 he worked at the Naval Examining Board in Washington, DC. He served as an Instructor in the Department of Marine Engineering at the United States Naval Academy from September 1937 to May 1939.

Sowell commanded the old Clemson-class destroyer USS *Decatur* (DD-341) from mid-1939 through December 1941. From September 1941 onward Sowell commanded *Decatur* during Neutrality Patrol duties, escorting convoys between the North American Coast and Iceland.

Following the United States' entry into World War II, Sowell left *Decatur*, briefly assigned to the Bureau of Navigation. On January 15, 1942, he took command of the Porter-class destroyer USS *Moffett* (DD-362). Sowell commanded *Moffett* for 18 months on anti-submarine patrol duties, mostly in the Caribbean and equatorial Atlantic waters east of Brazil. On May 17, 1943, *Moffett*, with Sowell commanding, participated in the sinking of the Type IXC U-boat *U-128* in Brazilian coastal waters, along with the Somers-class destroyer USS *Jouette* (DD-396) and two Martin PBM Mariner maritime patrol bombers from VP-74 Mariners. The Mariners depth-charged *U-128*, forcing it to the surface, where *Moffett* and *Jouette* sank it with gunfire. The destroyers captured 47 men of its crew, including its captain, Oberleutnant zur See Hermann Steinert.

Sowell was promoted to Captain in July 1943, leaving *Moffett*. Assuming command of Destroyer Division Thirty-Two in August, he conducted escort duties in the Atlantic and Mediterranean. He received a letter of commendation while performing escort duties in the Mediterranean on November 7, 1943. He was promoted to Commander, Escort US Atlantic Fleet in December 1943.

While commanding Convoy USG-40 from Norfolk to Naples, on May 11, 1944 the convoy came under an intense three-wave attack by German aircraft while in the Mediterranean. Sowell had given thought to a potential air attack while the convoy was at Norfolk, Virginia. He developed an air defense plan, practiced it four times in harbor, and every other day during passage across the Atlantic.

The German attack came while the convoy was six miles offshore, 100 miles east of Algiers, Algeria. Sowell's tactics resulted in downing nearly one-third of the 62 attacking bombers, while the Germans failed to score a single hit during the two-hour long attack. Convoy USG-40 arrived at Naples, Italy, having suffered no losses. Sowell was awarded a Legion of Merit, the first of three he received for anti-submarine actions protecting Atlantic convoys.

In September 1944 Sowell became the Assistant Operations officer for the US Atlantic Fleet, a position he held until September 1945. From September 1945 until July 1949 he served in the Office of the Chief of Naval Operations, Navy Department. After that he assumed command of the Oakland-class light cruiser USS *Juneau* (CLA-119), before being sent to the National War College in Washington, DC in February 1950. He died, age 74, on February 16, 1977.

Jesse Clyburn Sowell, United States Naval Academy yearbook photo. (AC)

WERNER HENKE

Werner Henke was one of the Kriegsmarine's top U-boat aces. In terms of total enemy tonnage sunk he ranked 12th with 155,714 tons sunk and 18th for the total number of ships sunk (24).

He was born on May 13, 1909, in Rudak, a small town outside Thorn, then part of Germany. His family moved to Celle, in Hannover to remain in Germany after Thorn became part of Poland in 1920. He joined the German merchant fleet as a young man.

In 1934, after several years as a merchant mariner, he joined the Reichsmarine, attending the Marineschule Mürwik (the Reichsmarine's and Kriegsmarine's Naval Academy in Flensberg, Germany). He served aboard the Deutschland-class *Panzerschiff* (armored ship) KMS *Deutschland* as a naval cadet. In October 1936 he was commissioned as a *Leutnant zur See* and served at the naval base at Pillau for two years being promoted to *Oberleutnant zur See* in June 1938. In May 1939 he was assigned to the old Deutschland-class battleship SMS *Schleswig-Holstein*, and participated in the bombardment of the Westerplatte at Danzig, Poland, where Germany fired the first shots of World War II.

He transferred to the U-boat service in April 1940, starting the six-week U-boat school. He failed to complete the course, being sent to a punishment unit after a conviction for desertion. Most probably, this was a case of overstaying a leave or being caught outside the base without leave, because in November 1940 he was assigned as an officer aboard Type IXB U-boat *U-124*.

U-124 was one of the Kriegsmarine's top U-boats, responsible for the sinking of 225,704 tons of shipping. Henke completed four war patrols on *U-124*, three under Korvettenkapitän Georg-Wilhelm Schulz and one under Korvettenkapitän Johann Mohr, both top U-boat aces credited with 89,886 tons and 135,751 tons of Allied shipping respectively. In November 1941 Henke was detached from *U-124* and sent to submarine commander's school.

On February 21, 1942, Henke commissioned *U-515*, a new Type IXC boat, with him in command. He would complete seven war patrols in *U-515*, in which he proceeded to outdo both of his prior commanders. Between September 1942 and January 1944, *U-515*, with Henke in command, sank 24 ships, and damaged four others, including one so badly it was a constructive total loss. This total included two warships sunk and one damaged.

On *U-515*'s seventh war patrol, ten days out of Lorient, France, it encountered Task Group 22.3 comprising five destroyer escorts and the Casablanca-class escort carrier USS *Guadalcanal* (CVE-60). Having found *U-515*, the U-boat hunter-killer group forced *U-515* to the surface on April 9, 1944 with an accurate depth-charge attack. Henke ordered the boat abandoned as it surfaced. Henke, along with 43 other survivors, became prisoners of war.

Captain Daniel V. Gallery, commanding Task Group 22.3, talked Henke into signing a statement agreeing to answer interrogation questions truthfully by threatening to give Henke to the British for trial as a war criminal. (Henke had sunk the 18,713-ton troopship *Ceramic* on the night of December 6/7, 1942, and was accused, falsely, of machine-gunning survivors.) Henke signed, but (as expected by Gallery) reneged on answering questions. Henke's signed agreement led other *U-515* crewmen to answer intelligence questions.

Either regretting signing the agreement or believing he would be turned over to the British for trial, Henke was killed attempting to escape from Fort Hunt, a prisoner-of-war camp in Virginia. He walked over to the fence in broad daylight, and slowly climbed it, ignoring guards' calls to stop. He died June 15, 1944, fatally shot. He was posthumously promoted to *Korvettenkapitän*.

Werner Henke as a *Kapitänleutnant*. (AC)

COMBAT

The crew of a US Navy destroyer set the depth-charge settings preparatory to dropping them on the suspected position of a U-boat. The proper depth had to be set for a depth charge to destroy a U-boat. (AC)

Combat between US Navy destroyers and destroyer escorts and German U-boats fell into several broad categories. It could occur while these warships were escorting convoys; a single warship might encounter a single U-boat; or a pack of destroyers, destroyer escorts, or a mix of these types in a carrier task group might encounter a U-boat while hunting for them.

The single-vessel encounter was the rarest. There was a lot of ocean and only chance led a lone U-boat to cross paths with a lone destroyer. Under those circumstances the U-boat would evade a single warship unless it managed to surprise the warship. Even when armed with homing torpedoes such encounters were perilous for a U-boat.

More common were encounters between US Navy warships escorting convoys and U-boats attacking them. Attacking merchant shipping was the U-boats' mission, and those ships were best found in convoys. Most convoy encounters occurred before mid-1942 or in the Mediterranean during 1943 and early 1944. Hunter-killer groups accounted for most encounters between US Navy destroyers and destroyer escorts and German U-boats, especially after mid-1943.

The four encounters described in this section include examples of all three types of encounters throughout the war. *Kearny*'s October 1941 fight with *U-568*, a convoy battle, occurred before the United States' entry into World War II. *Roper*'s April 1942 fight with *U-85* was a rare surface battle. *Eugene E. Elmore*'s May 1944 fight with *U-549* and *Farquhar*'s May 1945 fight with *U-881* introduce the destroyer escort and feature two different antisubmarine systems in the attacks: the Hedgehog and depth charges.

KEARNY VS *U-568* – OCTOBER 17, 1941

Convoy SC-48 was one convoy using the northern route across the Atlantic between Canada and Britain. It was an eastbound convoy for slow ships, those capable of maintaining a speed of less than 8kn. (Ships capable of making 9–13kn used faster HX convoys.) On October 5, 1941 the ships of SC-48 started out from Sydney, Canada, bound for Liverpool, England.

Because the ships were slow, and many of them elderly and unreliable, SC-48 was more likely to have ships straggle, making them easier for U-boats to catch. In 1941 these convoys – slow, vulnerable, and deeply laden with cargo bound for Britain – were considered prizes worth extra effort by the U-boat wolf packs. When the Germans discovered SC-48 on the morning of October 15, 1941, it was viewed as a priority U-boat target.

SC-48 departed Sydney with 52 merchantmen and eight escorts. German signal intelligence, reading the convoy code, knew when the convoy sailed. Dönitz set up a line of seven U-boats to find it. British intelligence learned the Germans were seeking SC-48 by reading German Enigma signal traffic, and they attempted to re-route SC-48 to avoid the U-boat line. Scattered by a storm between October 10 and 13, SC-48 had only 39 ships and four escorts (all corvettes) when discovered by Type VIIC *U-553* on the night of October 14/15. *U-553*, the southernmost U-boat in the line and a last-minute addition, attacked that morning, sinking two of SC-48's merchant ships, thus letting the British know SC-48 had been discovered.

Over the next day both sides gathered reinforcements. Guided by *U-553*, nine other U-boats moved to attack SC-48, movements captured by British codebreakers. Two Royal Navy destroyers and three corvettes from other convoys were sent to join SC-48.

More importantly, five US Navy destroyers – *Plunkett*, *Livermore*, *Kearny*, *Greer*, and *Decatur* – commanded by Captain Leo H. Thebaud, were sent. They had escorted HX-171 to the Mid-Ocean Meeting Point (MOMP) south of Iceland and were due to return escorting ON-24 heading to Canada. The first three were modern Gleaves-class destroyers; the other two were flush-deckers. *Greer* had tangled with a U-boat (*U-652*) only six weeks earlier.

This led to a massive convoy battle. Seven destroyers and seven corvettes represented the heaviest escort for a northern North Atlantic cargo convoy to date (troop convoys occasionally had heavier escorts). It should have been enough to deal with the ten U-boats converging on SC-48. Aircraft operating at maximum range from bases in Iceland kept the U-boats from attacking during the daylight hours, allowing for the reinforced escort to reach the beleaguered convoy; but as night fell, the aircraft had to return to base.

The United States was still neutral. However, since the declaration of the exclusion zone by President Roosevelt, US Navy warships had been escorting convoys from the

Convoy SC-48 on October 17. This photograph was taken from a Consolidated PBY Catalina from Iceland which airdropped blood plasma to USS *Kearny* (DD-432). Another Gleaves-class destroyer, either USS *Plunkett* (DD-431) or USS *Livermore* (DD-429), is in the foreground. (USNHHC)

MOMP west to Canada. Thebaud, as senior officer, was in charge of the escort. He had not been doing escort duty for very long.

Thebaud's inexperience led to problems. The escorts were kept close to the convoy – only 1,000–1,500yd from the outer columns. The QC sonar of the US Navy and the Type 124 sonar of the Royal Navy, the types then in service, had an effective range of 2,000–2,500yd. Under prevailing sea conditions it was probably less. The escorts were not equipped with radar. Once night fell, the U-boats could set up 4,000–5,000yd from the convoy – well within the 6,500yd maximum range of their torpedoes' fastest setting – and remain completely undetected.

That was what the U-boats did, remaining completely undetected. The convoy could be clearly seen from the U-boats' bridges, even during the dark, rainy night of October 16/17. They set up their shots unmolested. If two or three of the seven destroyers had been sent on roving patrols 1nm (6,076yd) from the convoy, the waiting "sea wolves" would have been discovered.

Possibly not. *U-553* remained surfaced, watching undetected as *Plunkett*, leading the convoy, passed within 160yd. Once inside the convoy, at 22:00:00 *U-553* fired three carefully aimed torpedoes at three different targets. Only one hit, sinking the 3,300-ton Panamanian freighter *Bold Venture*. Frustrated, Korvettenkapitän Karl Thurmann fired a fourth torpedo. It missed its intended target, but hit the Flower-class corvette HMS *Gladiolus*, a veteran and crack U-boat hunter with two confirmed and one probable U-boat kills. *Gladiolus* drifted dead in the water, eventually sinking.

The 22:00:00 attack was a signal for a general engagement to begin. At 23:15:00 Kapitänleutnant Heinz-Otto Schultze, commanding *U-432*, sank the 9,700-ton Norwegian tanker *Barfonn*, laden with aviation gasoline and the 5,283-ton Greek freighter *Evros* carrying iron ore. Two other torpedoes missed. At 23:50:00 on October

16, *U-558*, commanded by Kapitänleutnant Günther Krech, bagged two tankers: the 9,600-ton British *W.C. Teagle* and the 6,600-ton Norwegian *Erviken*. That attack probably also sank the 1,583-ton Norwegian steam merchant *Ila*, laden with steel. Escorts began steaming around the convoy, firing star shells and dropping depth charges. They did not hit any U-boats, but added considerably to the chaos of the sinkings.

While hunting U-boats, *Kearny* found the then-sinking *Gladiolus* dead ahead. *Kearny* backed engines to avoid colliding with the corvette, leaving the destroyer stopped in the middle of the battle. To *Kearny*'s right was *U-568*, commanded by Kapitänleutnant Joachim Preusse. Beyond *Kearny* on its left was *Barfonn*, its blazing aviation gasoline sending up a great column of flame, illuminating the convoy.

Flames etched *Kearny*'s silhouette against the sea. Preusse could not resist a perfect shot on an immobile hostile destroyer. He fired one G7 torpedo at the target. Shortly after midnight, just as October 17 began, the torpedo slammed into *Kearny*'s starboard side, just at the turn of the bilge. It hit just at the break of the forecastle, flooding the forward fireroom and destroying the No. 1 boiler.

The hit could have been fatal in an earlier destroyer design, as the next compartment – which would have also been a boiler room in previous designs – suffered damage sufficient to temporarily knock out those boilers as well, leaving *Kearny* powerless at a critical juncture. As it was, the forward engine shut down temporarily.

Kearny reached Reykjavik harbor two days after being torpedoed on October 17, 1941. The torpedo-hit can be seen under the break of the forecastle. Note that steam is coming only from the aft funnel. (USNHHC)

PREVIOUS PAGES

Battle between USS *Roper* and *U-85*

Shortly after midnight on April 14, 1942, the Clemson-class destroyer USS *Roper* found a contact with its newly installed radar. It was *U-85*, sent to attack shipping on the American Atlantic coast. In shallow water, unaware its foe had radar, *U-85* attempted to escape on the surface, using the darkness of night to shield it. Instead, like a greyhound hunting a rabbit, *Roper* charged down *U-85*, tracking it on radar. Desperate, *U-85*'s skipper fired a torpedo from *U-85*'s sole stern torpedo tube. It missed.

When *Roper* came within 300yd of *U-85*, the U-boat's captain ordered it be scuttled and abandoned. He threw the helm hard to starboard to avoid being rammed by *Roper*. The destroyer's captain interpreted the maneuver, and the sudden appearance of crewmen on *U-85*'s deck, as signs that they intended to man the deck guns and fight it out. *Roper*'s forward 24in searchlight blazed on and the destroyer opened up with every gun that would bear on *U-85*. This plate captures the battle at that point in time.

Kearny was steaming with her plant split, the forward boiler room feeding the forward engine and the after boiler room providing steam to the after engine. The loss of the forward fireroom led to the temporary loss of the starboard propeller, driven by the forward engine. The after plant continued running, however, providing power to run pumps and support damage control. After 15 minutes *Kearny* was steaming on the port screw, making 15kn.

Shortly after that, damage control isolated the forward fireroom from the forward engine room, setting up cross-connections to run the forward engine from the after fireroom. The torpedo blast had killed 11 and wounded another 22 crewmen, but the destroyer was able to reach Reykjavik, Iceland under its own power.

Later on October 17, British Escort Group 3 joined SC-48, adding four destroyers and several more corvettes and trawlers to the escort. Wolf pack Mordbrenner was able to pick off one more Royal Navy destroyer, HMS *Broadwater*, sunk by *U-101* that night, but was unable to further attack the merchantmen. In all, Convoy SC-48 lost nine of its merchantmen and two escorts, without a U-boat being sunk.

ROPER (DD-147) VS *U-85* – APRIL 14, 1942

In March 1942, Admiral Dönitz dispatched 20 Type VII U-boats to the American Atlantic coast. This was a follow-up to the spectacularly successful Operation *Paukenschlag* (Drumbeat) of January and February. For *Paukenschlag*, Dönitz sent nine Type IX U-boats to cruise the Atlantic coast. They sank over 30 ships without loss. Short of Type IXs and needing the few he had in the Caribbean and Gulf of Mexico, Dönitz sent two waves of Type VII U-boats on this March follow-up. *U-85* was one of them, dispatched with the second wave, leaving Saint-Nazaire, France on March 21.

U-85 was a Type VIIB U-boat, laid down on December 18, 1939, and on its fourth war patrol. Its captain, Oberleutnant zur See Eberhard Greger, had commanded it since its commissioning on June 7, 1941. An older Type VII, *U-85* was not a particularly successful U-boat. It had sunk only two ships on its previous three patrols, both during wolf-pack attacks on transatlantic convoys between Canada and Britain.

On its fourth patrol *U-85* was a lone raider, independently searching the American Atlantic coast between the Jersey Shore, New Jersey and Cape Hatteras, North Carolina. It arrived in American waters on April 7, 1942. Over the following week it sank just one ship, the 4,904-ton Norwegian motor freighter *Chr. Knudsen*, 50 miles east of Cape May, New Jersey.

Since that April 10 sinking *U-85* had been cruising down the Atlantic coast seeking other victims. As the sun set on April 13, Greger, taking advantage of a moonless night, positioned *U-85* in shallow waters near Bodie Island, north of Cape Hatteras. With the hull awash and only the small conning tower visible, the U-boat was nearly invisible to visual observation. It was a perfect spot to ambush shipping moving along the coast.

Earlier that day, USS *Roper* left Norfolk, Virginia steaming to an ASW patrol box off Cape Hatteras. *Roper*, a Wickes-class destroyer, was one of the flush-deck, four-pipe destroyers mass-produced at the end of World War I. It had been converted to ASW duties in 1940–41, re-armed with 3in/50 guns and K-guns augmenting its depth-charge racks. It spent the Neutrality Patrol months escorting Atlantic convoys, but had returned to Norfolk as 1942 opened. There it had been fitted with a British Type 286 meter-wave surface-search radar unit.

Shortly after midnight, *Roper*'s radar detected a contact at 2,700yd range. Lieutenant Commander Hamilton W. Howe chose to investigate, conning his destroyer closer to the contact. At that point, it was a routine contact in waters filled with other craft. Fishing boats, tugs, barges, salvage ships, and small craft were common. Boredom turned to excitement when *Roper*'s sonar room reported hearing fast screws. The contact was moving too quickly to be a fishing boat or a work boat. It was a possible warship, most likely a U-boat.

While a U-boat was invisible to the eye at nine-tenths of a nautical mile, at that distance, even on a moonless night, from the conning tower of the U-boat *Roper* was visible against the sky; but having spotted an enemy warship, possibly a destroyer to judge by its outline, Greger wanted to evade it. His position was ideal for ambushing freighters, but where he had set up for the night the sea bottom was only 100ft deep.

Greger had two choices: submerge in shallow water or make a high-speed surface run to deeper water. Submerged, he would be detectable by sonar in water so shallow as to make it impossible to avoid depth-charge damage. Surfaced he should remain invisible to lookouts if he kept *U-85*'s wake down.

Greger did not realize his opponent had radar – the Germans believed radar installations were too bulky and too delicate to install on destroyers – so he opted for the surface run. It seemed the safer. Two months earlier it would have worked, but *Roper*'s newly installed radar changed things. Once *U-85* started running, *Roper* knew the contact was a U-boat. It pursued.

The crew of *U-85* on deck as the U-boat leaves port, probably Lorient. *U-85* was sunk by the destroyer USS *Roper* (DD-147) while on its fourth patrol. This photo was found on the body of a *U-85* crewman after it was sunk, so it was taken prior to the fourth patrol. (USNHHC)

Roper in spring 1942. The destroyer had been converted to anti-submarine duty the previous year. Six 3in/50 guns replaced its 4in battery, with two of its triple torpedo tubes removed, and K-gun launchers and 20mm guns added. Note the radar antenna atop the foremast. (USNHHC)

OPPOSITE

The sinking of *U-549*

Type VIIB U-boats had a top surface speed of 17.9kn. After nearly a year at sea, however, *U-85*'s top speed was probably no greater than 16kn. *Roper* followed at 20kn. A stern chase is a long chase, but aided by its radar, *Roper* soon closed the 2,700yd gap between the two vessels. When they were 700yd apart Greger fired *U-85*'s stern torpedo tube in a final effort to shake off his pursuer.

The torpedo had a conventional warhead. The *Zaunkönig* acoustic homing torpedo would not be released for operational use for another year. Despite that, *U-85* came close to hitting *Roper*. The torpedo skimmed past the destroyer's port side, but *Roper* continued its relentless pursuit.

At 300yd *Roper* seemed ready to ram *U-85*. Greger ordered *U-85* scuttled, and its crew to abandon the U-boat. To avoid *Roper*'s oncoming bow, Greger swung *U-85* sharply to starboard.

When *U-85* turned, *Roper* turned on its forward 24in searchlight, illuminating the U-boat's conning tower and bridge. Spotting German sailors swarming out of the hatches, Howe concluded they were trying to man the U-boat's deck guns. *Roper* opened fire, raking *U-85* machine-gun and deck-gun fire. Meanwhile, *U-85* sank beneath its abandoning crew. They were left floundering in the water, shouting in German, "Please save us."

It was an opportunity for an intelligence coup. *U-85* went down in 98ft of water. Undamaged (it sank because its seacocks had been opened), it was within easy reach of divers. Inside the U-boat were its codebooks, operating manuals, and a four-rotor Enigma cipher machine. More could have been salvaged, including examples of the latest torpedoes. The crew could have been taken prisoner and interrogated.

Roper's crew were too excited by finally coming to grips with an enemy they had been vainly seeking for the last 90 days to consider this. Or, perhaps they were too new to war to realize the significance of their opportunity. When they saw *U-85* plunge below the surface, they assumed it was getting away.

U-85 is a war grave today, lying in the Monitor National Marine Sanctuary in Cape Hatteras, North Carolina. This is a composite photograph of *U-85* as it appears today. Its remains are considered too dangerous to enter. (NOAA)

Roper steamed over *U-85*'s last observed location and dropped 11 depth charges set to 50ft. The explosions shattered the U-boat, rolling it on its side, making its interior inaccessible to divers. *Roper*'s propellers chopped up some of the Germans in the water as the destroyer moved through them. The rest were killed by the depth-charge explosions. *Roper* stood away from the U-boat wreck until dawn, worried that *U-85* had a companion. Barely six weeks earlier *Jacob Jones*, another Wickes-class destroyer on anti-submarine patrol had been torpedoed and sunk off the New Jersey coast. *Roper* did not wish to suffer the same fate and returned only after daylight, accompanied by a heavy air escort. It found no survivors.

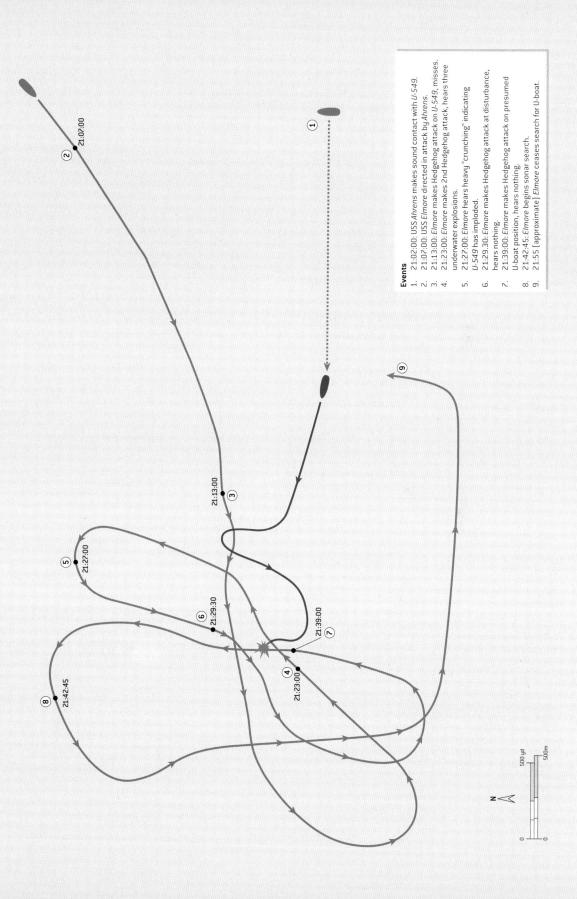

Events

1. 21:02:00: USS *Ahrens* makes sound contact with *U-549*.
2. 21:07:00: USS *Elmore* directed in attack by *Ahrens*.
3. 21:13:00: *Elmore* makes Hedgehog attack on *U-549*, misses.
4. 21:23:00: *Elmore* makes 2nd Hedgehog attack, hears three underwater explosions.
5. 21:27:00: *Elmore* hears heavy "crunching" indicating *U-549* has imploded.
6. 21:29:30: *Elmore* makes Hedgehog attack at disturbance, hears nothing.
7. 21:39:00: *Elmore* makes Hedgehog attack on presumed U-boat position, hears nothing.
8. 21:42:45: *Elmore* begins sonar search.
9. 21:55 (approximate) *Elmore* ceases search for U-boat.

The depth-charging was not – as one surviving U-boat captain implied after the war's end – a war crime. It *was* an intelligence blunder, however, that made the interior of the U-boat wreck inaccessible. This was overlooked in the good feeling that followed the US Navy's first successful kill of a German U-boat. Howe received a Navy Cross for the sinking of *U-85*.

EUGENE E. ELMORE (DE-686) VS *U-549* – MAY 29, 1944

In May 1943 the Battle of the Atlantic turned sharply against the U-boats. The Kriegsmarine lost 25 percent of its U-boat strength – 42 boats – in that disastrous month. It never recovered. Two months later Großadmiral (Grand Admiral) Dönitz withdrew his boats from the North Atlantic until improved weapons could be fielded. A year later, May 1944, U-boats were being dispatched to tie down Allied forces, but were being sent to remote patrol areas. *U-549* was one of them.

U-549 was a long-range Type IXC/40 U-boat, one of the vessels retrofitted with a Schnorchel. Commanded by Kapitänleutnant Detlev Krankenhagen, *U-549* left the U-boat base at Lorient on May 14, 1944. It was the U-boat's second war patrol. It sank nothing on its first patrol, a futile 76-day cruise across the northern transatlantic convoy routes to Britain. This time it was bound for a patrol off Brazil.

U-549's departure had been noted by Allied intelligence. Codebreakers, decrypting orders radioed to *U-549*, concluded it was being sent on a special mission, possibly to Argentina to deliver spies and radio equipment. While this assessment was wrong (*U-549* was on a routine patrol) it triggered a massive hunt to prevent completion of its mythical mission.

Task Group 21.11, consisting of the Bogue-class escort carrier USS *Block Island* (CVE-21) and Escort Division (Cortdiv) 60 (Buckley-class destroyer escorts USS *Ahrens* (DE-575), USS *Barr* (DE-576), and USS *Robert I. Paine* (DE-578), and Rudderow-class destroyer escort USS *Eugene E. Elmore* (DE-686)), was operating off the Cape Verde islands in the central Atlantic. *Block Island*, 16,620 tons and capable of 18kn, was carrying nine Grumman Wildcat fighters and 12 radar-equipped Grumman Avenger torpedo bombers. *Ahrens*, *Barr*, and *Robert I. Paine* had main batteries of three 3in/50 guns; *Eugene E. Elmore* had two 5in/38 guns, but was otherwise identical to the other three ships. Since TG21.11 was near *U-549*'s expected path, it was directed to stop the U-boat.

On May 23, TG 21.11 began an intense air search for *U-549*. Avengers from *Block Island*'s VC-55 made radar contact with the U-boat on May 28; but the contact was brief, lost before *U-549* could be attacked. Another contact occurred at 02:55:00 on May 29, but *U-549* submerged before it could be attacked. TG 21.11 intensified its search for the U-boat over the course of the day. At one point 13 of VC-55's 21 aircraft were airborne, seeking *U-549*, but it continued to evade its pursuers.

On the evening of May 29, *U-549* found TG 21.11. At 20:15:00, an hour before sunset, *U-549* struck. Running submerged at periscope depth, it launched a spread of four torpedoes at *Block Island*. It is probable that these were FAT torpedoes fitted with a spring mechanism that caused the torpedo to loop back after following a preset straight course. Three hit the escort carrier: two at 20:03:00, during the straight run, the fourth 20 minutes later at 20:23:00, almost certainly during a return loop.

Mortally wounded, *Block Island* began sinking. *Barr*, seeing *U-549*'s periscope, made a run on the U-boat, dropping 11 depth charges. All 11 missed, and as *U-549* dove, Krankenhagen fired a *Zaunkönig* acoustic homing torpedo at *Barr*. It hit the destroyer escort near the stern. The damaged *Barr* was immobilized, but did not sink.

Meanwhile *U-549* went deep, probably to its test depth, below the maximum depth setting of US depth charges. In the turmoil following the torpedoing of *Block Island* and *Barr*, surviving ships of TG 21.11 lost contact with the U-boat.

Ahrens and *Robert I. Paine* began the task of rescuing survivors from *Block Island*, moving slowly to recover men from the water. *Ahrens* stopped its engines to recover sailors. At 21:02:00, with engines off and the ship quiet, *Ahrens* picked up *U-549* on its sonar bearing 275 degrees from *Ahern*'s bow.

Barr was damaged, dead in the water. *Ahrens* and *Robert I. Paine* were rescuing survivors. *Eugene E. Elmore* was the only available ship. Lieutenant Commander Morgan H. Harris, captain of *Ahrens*, directed *Eugene E. Elmore*, commanded by Lieutenant Commander George L. Conkey, to the contact, which it soon found with its sonar.

The rest of the battle unfolded quickly. *U-549* was deep, running as silently as it could. Krankenhagen probably thought he was safe because detection was difficult at that depth. He did not have to worry about depth charges because *U-549* was below

U-549 turned the tables on TG 21.11 when it torpedoed the Bogue-class escort carrier USS *Block Island* (CVE-21) on May 29, 1944. The escort carrier is shown sinking by the stern in this photograph, probably taken from the Buckley-class destroyer escort USS *Ahrens* (DE-575). (USNHHC)

the level at which they were effective. He just had to wait until the Americans lost contact or got tired of making futile attacks.

Krankenhagen had two problems, however. First, *Eugene E. Elmore* was fitted with an extremely sensitive Type 144 sonar. Its normal range was 2,500yd. Under ideal conditions, it could detect a U-boat 3,000yd distant. Having locked onto *U-549*, *Eugene E. Elmore* was unlikely to lose it. Second, the sonar was integrated into the fire control of *Eugene E. Elmore*'s Hedgehog projector. Hedgehog projectiles were not depth-fused; they had contact fuses. They dropped until they hit something, regardless of depth.

Moving slowly enough to prevent noise from breaking sonar contact, at 21:13:00 *Eugene E. Elmore* made a Hedgehog run. Aware of the destroyer escort's presence through its hydrophones, *U-549* turned 180 degrees to port, probably timing the maneuver to match the sonar blind spot during a depth-charge run. The projectiles missed their intended target, silently sinking to the ocean floor.

Eugene E. Elmore maintained sonar contact with *U-549*, reloading its Hedgehog with 24 more projectiles. It came around to *U-549*'s position a second time, firing the Hedgehog again. Just over 30 seconds later, three underwater explosions were heard, indicating three of the 24 projectiles had found *U-549*. Four minutes later, *Eugene E. Elmore* picked up the sound of a heavy crunching "explosion."

It was more likely the sound of *U-549* imploding as it reached crush depth. The U-boat had been destroyed. If its crew were lucky, one of the three projectiles had opened the pressure hull, killing all inside instantly. If the projectiles had just opened the ballast tanks without rupturing the pressure hull, *U-549* would have started

The Rudderow-class destroyer escort USS *Eugene E. Elmore* (DE-686) as it appeared in May 1944. It executed four Hedgehog attacks on *U-549* on May 29, 1944, almost certainly sinking it with the second attack. (NARA)

INTEGRATING THE BATTLE SYSTEM

Germany and the United States both entered World War II with warships fighting traditionally. The captain directed the battle, gunners (or torpedomen or depth-charge teams) fired the weapons, while those operating sensors – rangefinders, radar, and sonar – sent targeting information to the weapons. Centralized fire control was state of the art. The Kriegsmarine never progressed much beyond that, especially on their U-boats. It worked. The skipper handled everything from the conning tower.

The number and complexity of different sensor and weapons systems aboard a warship, even small destroyers, meant the old approach failed to produce top performance in combat – and combat's award for second place was often a sunken ship.

The US Navy looked for ways to get all systems working better together, which led to development of the Combat Information Center. The captain remained on the bridge directing the battle, but a subordinate, generally a destroyer's executive officer, would be in a separate room to which all relevant information was sent. This improved combat performance. By 1944, systems were further integrated. Leading-edge sonars and radars fed targeting

information directly to the weapons, contributing to the dramatic improvement in Hedgehog accuracy from mid-1944 onward.

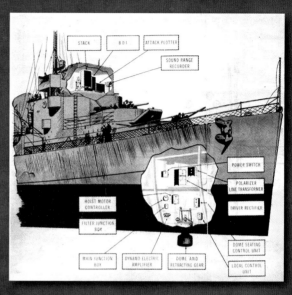

A diagram showing how sonar readings are integrated into the Combat Information Center. (AC)

plunging to the ocean bottom. The crew would have had four interminable minutes of waiting before the pressure hull finally yielded.

Eugene E. Elmore's captain was not completely satisfied that *U-549* was dead, so the destroyer escort made two more runs at *U-549*, firing two more Hedgehog salvoes, using the roiling waters marking the site of the underwater explosions as the aiming point on the first run and the crossed wakes of its previous two attempts for the second.

Nothing was heard either time. *Eugene E. Elmore* slowly circled, sweeping the area with its sonar, seeking any trace of a U-boat. The results were negative. *Eugene E. Elmore* finally gave up the search shortly before *Block Island* finally sank at 21:58:00. By then night had fallen and *Ahrens* and *Robert I. Paine* had recovered 951 of the 957 men aboard *Block Island* when *U-549* torpedoed it.

Ahrens and *Robert I. Paine* spent the rest of the night searching for submarines, but found nothing. *Eugene E. Elmore* went to assist *Barr*, taking aboard 14 wounded and any crew deemed unnecessary to salvaging *Barr*. Damage-control parties patched the leaks, and *Eugene E. Elmore* took *Barr* under tow. The four destroyer escorts and *Block Island*'s survivors reached Casablanca, Morocco, three days later.

Barr was patched up, converted to a fast destroyer transport (APD) and saw service in the Pacific in 1945. Most of *Block Island*'s crew stayed together. They ended up assigned to a new *Block Island* (CVE-106), a Commencement Bay-class escort carrier, renamed for the sunken vessel. *U-549* was never heard of again, presumed sunk by *Eugene E. Elmore*.

FARQUHAR (DE-139) VS *U-881* – MAY 6, 1945

Upon Adolf Hitler's death on April 30, 1945, Dönitz was named his successor, becoming Reichsführer Dönitz. He delayed surrendering the Reich until May 8, to permit evacuation of German nationals and military personnel fleeing the Soviets (a seaborne operation that continued, with Field Marshall Bernard Montgomery's tacit permission, until May 9). On May 4, Dönitz issued an order for all Kriegsmarine warships to cease offensive operations. On May 5 he sent a message ordering all U-boats at sea to immediately cease all hostilities.

There is always someone who does not get the word – or, if they get it, chooses to ignore it. Such was the case with *U-853* and *U-881*. Both were Schnorchel-equipped Type IXC/40 U-boats, two of nine Schnorchel U-boats dispatched in April 1945 as part of Operation *Seewolf*, part of a last-ditch U-boat offensive along the American Atlantic Coast.

These nine U-boats represented a maximum effort. All had orders to cross the Atlantic submerged and mount a coordinated offensive in the last week of April, a reprise of 1942's Operation *Paukenschlag*. Allied signal intelligence detected messages about the operation, but not its purpose (a conventional attack on what the Germans hoped was unwary merchant shipping). Operation *Seewolf* made little sense militarily. Rather, it was the best the Kriegsmarine could do to distract the Allies from operations in Germany itself.

U-805 was one of nine Type IXC and Type IXC/40 U-boats sent to attack shipping off the American Atlantic seaboard during Operation *Seewolf*. The US Navy's Operation *Teardrop* destroyed all but two of the Operation *Seewolf* U-boats. *U-805* was one of the two survivors. (USNHHC)

U-881 encountered the Casablanca-class escort carrier *USS Mission Bay* (CVE-59) on May 6, 1945 when the *Mission Bay* Task Group was returning to Norfolk, Virginia after Operation *Teardrop*. *U-881* was attempting to torpedo *Mission Bay* when the U-boat itself was sunk. (USNHHC)

They succeeded in eliciting an Allied response, but not the response for which they had hoped. Allied intelligence, unable to find a conventional objective justifying the German effort, decided a more unconventional objective was the goal. Intelligence was convinced the U-boats had been converted to launch V-1 or V-2 missiles for a concerted strike on American Atlantic coast cities. In response Operation *Teardrop* was mounted.

Two barriers were raised across the center of the North Atlantic through which U-boats operating from Norwegian ports had to pass to reach American coastal waters. Each was anchored by escort carrier task groups at its northern and southern boundaries. Forty miles ahead, a line of destroyer escorts was positioned at five-mile or ten-mile intervals to detect snorting U-boats. The eastern gauntlet, just west of Iceland, had the Casablanca-class escort carrier *Mission Bay* and the Bogue-class escort carrier USS *Croatan* (CVE-25). The western gauntlet, located east of the Grand Banks, Canada, used the Bogue-class escort carriers USS *Core* (CVE-13) and USS *Bogue* (CVE-9).

Two of Operation *Seewolf's* U-boats were sunk by RAF Coastal Command aircraft departing Norway. A third U-boat returned to port. Destroyer escorts participating in Operation *Teardrop* sank four of the remaining seven U-boats. Three U-boats, *U-853*, *U-858*, and *U-805*, slipped through the net. A fourth, *U-881*, evaded detection because it returned to port for repairs and departed late.

Following Dönitz's messages of May 4 and 5, the Operation *Teardrop* forces began returning to Norfolk. Two of the surviving four U-boats, *U-858* and *U-805* followed orders. They found a patch of sea and hid. *U-853* and *U-881* did not. They had either ignored or not received Dönitz's May 4 order to cease offensive operations, or his May 5 order to cease combat operations. Running submerged, Schnorchel-equipped U-boats found radio communications difficult.

Regardless, both continued fighting. *U-853* was caught near Block Island, New York by US Navy ASW forces on May 5, shortly after sinking the collier *Black Point*, bound for Boston. Trapped on the bottom it was sunk at 23:37:00 by a Hedgehog barrage delivered by the Cannon-class destroyer escort USS *Atherton* (DE-169). Except for the depth involved it was similar to *Eugene E. Elmore*'s attack that destroyed *U-549* a year earlier.

The final encounter between US Navy destroyers and destroyer escorts and Kriegsmarine U-boats occurred two hours later. The tardy *U-881* encountered the *Mission Bay* Task Group off Grand Banks as the task group was returning to Norfolk. It was a chance meeting. *U-881* had sailed March 19 but experienced Schnorchel problems. Having returned to Bergen, Norway on March 30 for repairs, it resumed its mission April 7, once the problem was fixed.

Kapitänleutnant Dr. Karl-Heinz Frischke maintained radio silence for the next 29 days. Whether voluntarily or possibly due to equipment failure, there was no recorded radio traffic between U-boat headquarters and *U-881* during its voyage. As a result, *U-881* had evaded the codebreakers and missed getting caught in either of the two barriers.

The next contact with *U-881* occurred in the pre-dawn hours of May 6, 1945, some 36 hours after Dönitz had broadcast his order to cease offensive operations and 12 hours after his order to cease all combat operations. *U-881* found itself in a position dreamed of by every U-boat captain since 1943 – perfectly placed to sink an Allied aircraft carrier. Through ignorance or defiance *U-881* began lining up an attack on *Mission Bay* in what promised to be a repeat of *Block Island*'s sinking in May 1944.

Block Island's screen had been short one destroyer escort when it encountered *U-549*. By contrast, *Mission Bay* was accompanied by six destroyer escorts in May 1945. One, USS *Farquhar*, spotted a U-boat's periscope as *U-881* lined up its shot on *Mission Bay*. It was the first indication there was a U-boat in the vicinity. No sound contact had been reported prior to spotting the periscope. Possibly *U-881* had been running on its batteries as the racket made by a diesel engine in a submerged U-boat was detectable for miles on destroyer escort's hydrophones. Alternatively, a combination of water conditions and the task group's speed could have prevented hydrophone or sonar detection. Regardless, *Mission Bay* was in deadly peril.

Without waiting to call *Farquhar*'s captain, the officer of the watch, Lieutenant Lloyd R. Borst, launched an immediate attack. Bringing *Farquhar* to full ahead, he charged over to where the periscope had been sighted. *U-881* dived as soon as Frischke realized it was being attacked, but dived too late. At 04:41:00 on May 6, Borst made a perfectly laid depth-charge attack, dropping a pattern of 13 depth charges set to shallow depths.

The method of attack was almost anachronistic. Since sinking *U-549*, Hedgehog projectiles had accounted for most U-boat kills made by destroyer escorts. In 1945 the Hedgehog projector was the destroyer escort's weapon of choice against the U-boat.

Borst's instinctive choice to attack with depth charges was correct. His intention was as much to break up the attack on *Mission Bay* as to sink a U-boat. A Hedgehog projectile would not explode unless it hit something, whereas depth charges automatically exploded when they reached their depth setting. Even if the depth charges missed, the explosions would shake up the U-boat.

The attack did not miss. The depth charges landed close enough to finish *U-881*. It plunged to the bottom taking all aboard with it. It was the last US Navy anti-submarine action of the Battle of the Atlantic.

ANALYSIS

During the 44 months in which US Navy fought Kriegsmarine U-boats, the destroyers and destroyer escorts of the US Navy sank 22 Type IX U-boats, ten Type VII U-boats, and three Type X and Type XIV supply boats. The U-boats sank four flush-deck destroyers, three destroyer escorts, one Sims-class destroyer, and one Gleaves-class destroyer. Breaking down these losses by year yields the following:

Year	Destroyers Sunk	Destroyer Escorts Sunk	Type VII U-boats Sunk	Type IX U-boats	Other U-boats Sunk	Total U-boats Sunk
1941	1					
1942	1		1	1		2
1943	4		3	4		7
1944		2	5	8*	3	16
1945		1	1	9		10

* Includes one captured.

The data shows several trends. The US Navy destroyer force sank over twice as many Type IX U-boats (of all variants) as they did Type VII U-boats. However, the Kriegsmarine commissioned and built these U-boats in almost exactly the opposite ratio: 693 Type VIIs of all variants and 193 Type IXs. US Navy destroyers and destroyer escorts accounted for roughly 1.5 percent of the Type VII U-boats commissioned by the Kriegsmarine, 11 percent of the Type IX U-boats commissioned by the Kriegsmarine, and 19 percent of the supply boats commissioned.

Kriegsmarine *U-bootsmänner* starting a patrol. A total of 37,000 men served on U-boats, 28,000 of whom died or were declared missing. A further 5,000 men were taken prisoner. Including those captured, U-boat personnel suffered 90 percent casualties, three-quarters of whom died. (USNHHC)

US Navy destroyers and destroyer escorts did most of their killing in the last 18 months of the war. They sank no U-boats in 1941, prior to the United States' entry into the war (despite losing the destroyer *Reuben James* in 1941). They accounted for nine U-boats in the 24 months of 1942 and 1943, and 26 from January 1944 through May 1945.

Some of that is attributable to more resources being available in 1944 and 1945. Production of destroyers and destroyer escorts skyrocketed in the war's early years, rising by a factor of nearly ten between 1941 and 1943. This included the new destroyer escorts intended to hunt U-boats. The first contracts for these were let in November 1941, but the first vessels did not see combat until April 1943. Before 1943 ended so many had been built or were under construction the US Navy canceled construction of nearly half the vessels ordered and converted nearly one-third of those retained to other duties.

Technology was another reason for US Navy success. In 1941 no US destroyer on anti-submarine duty was equipped with surface-search radar. *Roper*, one of the first such in the Atlantic to be so equipped, immediately proved its worth, finding and sinking *U-85* on its first patrol with a functioning radar. By mid-1943 most destroyers and all destroyer escorts in the Atlantic had surface-search radar. Similarly, most were equipped with HF/DF by then and all had it by 1944.

Improved weapons helped. Until August 1942 when a 600ft maximum depth setting of US Navy depth charges replaced the pre-war 300ft setting, U-boats could easily dive below the maximum setting, and wait out a depth-charge attack with impunity. At the 600ft setting, Type VII and Type IX U-boats could dive to their 230m (750ft) test depth, their conning tower some 60ft below the 600ft line – safely below the maximum kill radius of even a 600lb depth charge.

The anti-submarine projectile, introduced in 1943, led to massive improvement in ASW effectiveness. It had no effective maximum depth. It could also be fired while in sonar contact with a U-boat, and made no noise until it made physical contact with a U-boat. U-boats hiding at test depth could now be reached, and the effectiveness of the attack could be assessed almost immediately. A methodical Hedgehog attack, such as that mounted by *Eugene E. Elmore* against *U-549* on May 29, 1944, was almost always successful. One downside, however, was that Hedgehog projectors were not typically mounted on destroyers assigned to ASW duties in the Atlantic, only destroyer escorts. Additionally, the Hedgehog projector required a well-trained crew for effective use. Of the last 16 sinkings of U-boats by US Navy destroyers and destroyer escorts in World War II, 11 were achieved using projectiles rather than depth charges.

The biggest factors in improved ASW performance were experience and tactics. Early US Navy ASW tactics for destroyers were fatally flawed. The battle fought around Convoy SC-48 on October 16/17, 1941 demonstrated the danger of keeping escorts close to a convoy in predictable positions. Another lesson learned was the folly of responding to a U-boat attack by randomly dropping depth charges. Doing this confused situational awareness without improving the chances of sinking a U-boat.

A strong escort combined with aggressive patrolling by the escorts and disciplined use of depth charges could successfully defeat even a large wolf-pack attack on a convoy. The US Navy took the lessons learned from the Convoy SC-48 attack to heart, applying those rules thereafter. This was one reason no convoy escorted by a primarily US Navy warship escort ever lost five or more ships. (In fairness, this led to increased merchant ship casualties elsewhere. The philosophy that a "weak escort is worse against wolf packs than no convoy" led to fewer convoys and more individual sailings in 1942. This led to massive losses of merchant ships to U-boats operating independently.)

The US Navy spent much of 1942 randomly seeking U-boats with its destroyers in 1942. It only found and sank one that way, when *Roper* stumbled across *U-85*.

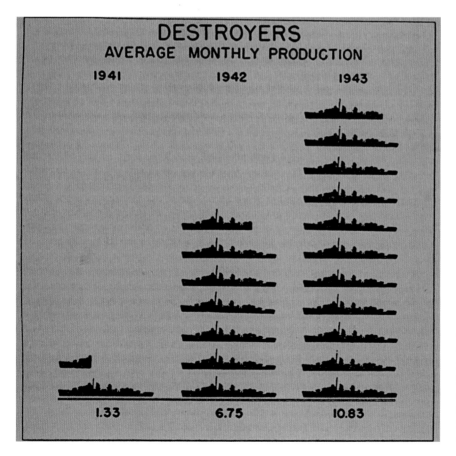

By 1943 nearly 11 US Navy destroyers or destroyer escorts were being commissioned each month. Rates increased as 1944 began, but production was eventually slashed when it became obvious there would be more vessels, especially destroyer escorts, than needed. (AC)

(The other, Type IXC *U-173*, was sunk attacking the heavily escorted Operation *Torch* shipping in November 1942.) Those patrols demonstrated there was simply too much ocean to find a U-boat by randomly patrolling destroyers. Not until the US Navy deployed hunter-killer teams in fall 1943 did the number of U-boats sunk dramatically increase.

The combination of Allied intelligence, carrier aircraft search and attack, and destroyers or destroyer escorts dedicated to the destruction of U-boats proved fatal for the U-boats' fortunes. Four of the seven U-boats sunk by destroyers or destroyer escorts in 1943 were sunk by vessels in hunter-killer groups. A further ten U-boats were sunk by hunter-killer groups in 1944 and eight in 1945.

While destroyers hunted U-boats, U-boats were better off avoiding destroyers. Picking a fight with a destroyer, especially a destroyer escort, was ill-advised. These small, agile vessels were almost impossible to hit with conventional steam or electric torpedoes if they were maneuvering. If a U-boat were in the presence of a destroyer which was aware of the U-boat, an immediate dive to 230m (750ft) was safer than a down-the-throat torpedo shot at an onrushing destroyer.

The only US Navy destroyers sunk by U-boats using standard torpedoes were *Reuben James* in October 1941 and *Jacob Jones* in February 1942. In these cases, as well

US Navy destroyers and destroyer escorts proved tough ships. One torpedo did not guarantee a sinking. This is *Kearny* photographed at Reykjavik after being torpedoed by *U-568*. (USNHHC)

as the torpedoing of *Kearny* by *U-568* in October 1941 and the Gleaves-class destroyer USS *Hambleton* (DD-455) by *U-173* in November 1942, the attacks were ambushes. The undetected U-boats were allowed carefully aimed shots at destroyers sailing straight or nearly stopped.

The few occasions U-boats fought it out with an attacking destroyer using conventional torpedoes ended badly for the U-boat. *U-85*'s attempt to torpedo *Roper* was a typical outcome. Of course, *U-85* had no other card to play. It was in water too shallow to escape by diving.

All but one of the remaining destroyers and destroyer escorts sunk in battles with U-boats were sunk by a *Zaunkönig* acoustic homing torpedo. Even that was dicey. The *Zaunkönig* was ineffective if the target was traveling under 10kn or over 18kn. A destroyer going at flank speed would likely be missed. Additionally, destroyers could deploy a "foxer" – a noisemaker to draw the *Zaunkönig* away from the destroyer's propellers.

Under the right circumstances, the *Zaunkönig* torpedoes were effective. Usually they would blow the stern off the victim. More rarely, as with *Frederick C. Davis*, sunk in April 1945, it would hit amidships. Yet, unless the target was operating individually, even a successful attack could lead to the U-boat's destruction. *U-546* was hunted to the death after sinking *Frederick C. Davis* by the surviving destroyer escorts in the screen, much as *Eugene E. Elmore* avenged *Block Island* by sinking *U-549*. Additionally, a single torpedo hit rarely sank anything but a flush-deck destroyer.

The final vessel lost to U-boats was *Borie*, which sank due to damage incurred by ramming *U-405*. It was a method only satisfying if you belonged to the "take one with you" school of warfare. Ramming was generally inadvisable as a method of destroying U-boats or destroyers because it led to damage to both the initiator and the victim.

The aforementioned loss numbers do not seem like large totals. Germany lost 768 U-boats to all causes, including accidents, 710 of these after the US officially entered World War II. That means only 5 percent of all U-boats lost were accounted for by the destroyers and destroyer escorts of the US Navy. Similarly, of the 71 US Navy-manned destroyers and ten destroyer escorts lost during World War II, U-boats sank nine – just over 13 percent.

They represented a major effort for both sides, however. That the numbers were so low is more an indicator of the late arrival of the United States into World War II. It is also due to the changing nature of the Battle of the Atlantic. By 1943, when the US Navy arrived in force in the Atlantic, the biggest U-boat killer had become the ASW aircraft.

Additionally, geography dictated that the US Navy would play a supporting role in ASW in the Atlantic. U-boats had to run a gauntlet of Allied air forces and Royal Navy warships to reach the areas where the US Navy generally operated. This was one reason the ratios of Type VII and Type IX U-boats built and Type VII and Type IX U-boats sunk by US Navy destroyers and destroyer escorts were nearly reverse. The long-range Type IXs were more likely to encounter US Navy destroyers than the shorter-legged Type VIIs, especially after the supply boats the Type VIIs depended upon for mid-ocean replenishment were destroyed.

AFTERMATH

Germany officially surrendered on May 8, 1945. The Allies immediately broadcast an order for all U-boats at sea to surface, fly a black flag or pennant, report their position to the nearest Allied radio station, and obey orders received to complete their surrender. All but two of the 49 U-boats then at sea complied with the Allies' order. Most were in waters for which the Royal Navy held responsibility. As a result, very few surrendered to the US Navy.

The two surviving boats from Operation *Seewolf*, *U-805* and *U-858*, were among those that surrendered. Both surfaced on May 9 as directed, but had to wait several days before rendezvousing with their captors. *U-805* surrendered off Cape Race, Canada, on May 13; *U-858* off the Delaware Capes on May 14. They were joined by Type IXD2 *U-873* on May 16, and Type X *U-234* on May 19. That was it.

U-873 had been patrolling the southern American Atlantic coast independently from the Operation *Seewolf* U-boats, but had found nothing. It, too, survived by maintaining radio silence and not finding any targets worth attacking. Otherwise it would likely have shared the fates of *U-853* and *U-881*. The US Navy had plenty of resources available to give U-boats its concentrated attention once discovered.

U-234 had a more interesting tale. It departed Kristiansand, Norway, on April 16, bound for Japan. A cargo U-boat, it was carrying a load of uranium oxide and high-tech German weapons to the Japanese. Also aboard were two Japanese officers. On May 14, having complied with Dönitz's orders to surface and surrender, its uranium oxide was seized and allegedly sent to the Manhattan Project's diffusion plant at Oak Ridge, Tennessee, for processing. The refined uranium possibly was included in the two atomic bombs dropped on Japan in August 1945. If so, it reached its original destination in a most unconventional manner.

U-858 arriving at Cape Henlopen, Delaware after surrendering to the US Navy on May 14, 1945. The boat is manned by US Navy personnel. Note the Sikorsky HNS-1 helicopter and the blimp. (USNHHC)

The U-boats, destroyers, and destroyer escorts that participated in the Battle of the Atlantic were largely retired once the war ended. Most of the U-boats and pre-war destroyers were scrapped in 1946–48. A few U-boats served in the Soviet, French, and Norwegian navies in the 1940s and 1950s, but none were preserved afterward. *U-505*, a Type IXC captured on June 4, 1944, survived as a war prize, and is on display at the Chicago Museum of Science and Industry.

The Gleaves-class destroyers and the destroyer escorts remained in reserve fleets for a few years after that, but they too ended up being scrapped in the decades after World War II. No destroyer that fought in the Battle of the Atlantic was preserved. Only two destroyer escorts now remain as museum ships in the United States, and perhaps five others are scattered over the rest of the globe.

In the post-war years, scuba diving became a popular sport worldwide. Most of the wrecks sank in water too deep for even professional divers, but a few, including those of *Jacob Jones*, *U-85*, and *U-853*, sank in shallow waters off the American Atlantic seaboard. These, especially *U-85*, are popular dive destinations today. All are protected as war graves.

FURTHER READING

Any book featuring the Battle of the Atlantic has to draw on a wide variety of sources, but they are too numerous for me to list all of them. I have listed the most important below. Additional sources can be found in other Osprey books I have written that have touched on the Battle of the Atlantic, most notably the New Vanguards about flush-deck destroyers and destroyer escorts, the two-part Air Campaign about the air phase of the Battle of the Atlantic, and the Raid on the capture of *U-505*.

For the battles described in this book, I have relied heavily on both volumes of Clay Blair's excellent *Hitler's U-Boat War* and the two volumes of Samuel Eliot Morison's 15-volume *History of United States Naval Operations in World War II* which focused on the Battle of the Atlantic. They occasionally contradict each other in details and conclusions, but are valuable, especially when combined with the actual action reports for the various battles.

The Friedman and Polmar titles listed provide a wealth of technical data, as do the numerous US Navy publications I used detailing everything from how to operate depth charges to navy recipes. There was also much to be found on several online websites about the Battle of the Atlantic, U-boats, and naval weapons. These include:

http://www.navweaps.com/

http://www.convoyweb.org.uk/

http://destroyerhistory.org/

https://uboat.net/

The main books I used were (books marked with an asterisk are available online):

Blair, Clay, *Hitler's U-Boat War: The Hunters, 1939–1942*, Random House, New York, NY, 1992

Blair, Clay, *Hitler's U-Boat War: The Hunted, 1942–1945*, Random House, New York, NY, 1992

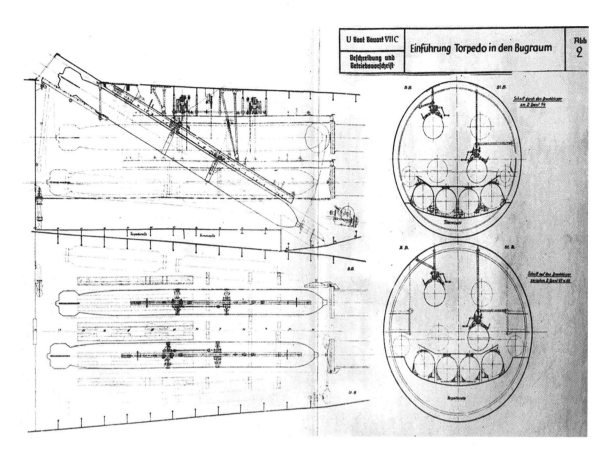

A page from a Kriegsmarine technical manual captured by the US Navy. It shows how torpedoes were loaded into and stored in the forward torpedo room of a Type VII U-boat. (AC)

Friedman, Norman, *Naval Radar*, Naval Institute Press, Annapolis, MD, 1981

Friedman, Norman, *U.S. Destroyers: An Illustrated Design History*, Naval Institute Press, Annapolis, MD, 1989

King, Ernest J., *U.S. Navy at War 1941–1945: Official Reports to the Secretary of the Navy*, United States Navy Department, Washington, DC, 1946*

Meier, Friedrich, *Kriegsmarine am Feind*, Verlag Erich Klingmammer, Berlin, 1940*

Morison, Samuel Eliot, *History of United States Naval Operations in World War II, Volume 1: The Battle of the Atlantic, September 1939–May 1943*, Little, Brown, Boston, MA, 1946

Morison, Samuel Eliot, *History of United States Naval Operations in World War II, Volume 10: The Atlantic Battle Won, May 1943–May 1945*, Little, Brown, Boston, MA, 1956

Polmar, Norman and Edward, Whitman, *Hunters and Killers, Volume 1: Anti-Submarine Warfare from 1776 to 1943*, Naval Institute Press, Annapolis, MD, 2015

Polmar, Norman and Edward, Whitman, *Hunters and Killers, Volume 2: Anti-Submarine Warfare from 1943*, Naval Institute Press, Annapolis, MD, 2016

United States Navy, *The Bluejackets' Manual 1940, Tenth Edition*, United States Naval Institute, Annapolis, MD, 1940

Williamson, Gordon, *German Seaman 1939–45*, Osprey Publishing, Oxford, 2009

An official online source used was:

Dictionary of American Naval Fighting Ships, online edition: https://www.history.navy.mil/research/histories/ship-histories/danfs.html

INDEX